M000223473

ECCLESIASTES: LIFE IN THE LIGHT OF ETERNITY

David Gibson

STUDY GUIDE WITH LEADER'S NOTES

New
Growth
Press

newgrowthpress.com

New Growth Press, Greensboro, NC 27404
newgrowthpress.com
Copyright © 2021 by David Gibson

All rights reserved. No part of this publication may be reproduced, stored in a retrieval system, or transmitted in any form by any means, electronic, mechanical, photocopy, recording, or otherwise, without the prior permission of the publisher, except as provided by USA copyright law.

This study guide follows the author's approach to Ecclesiastes in his book *Destiny: Learning to Live by Preparing to Die* (IVP, 2016) and published in the USA as *Living Life Backward: How Ecclesiastes Teaches Us to Live in Light of the End* (Crossway, 2017). Some of the material also first appeared on the Desiring God website and is used with permission.

Scripture quotations are from The ESV˚ Bible (The Holy Bible, English Standard Version˚), copyright © 2001 by Crossway, a publishing ministry of Good News Publishers. Used by permission. All rights reserved.

Cover Design: Faceout Books, faceoutstudio.com
Interior Design and Typesetting: Gretchen Logterman
Exercises and Application Questions: Jack Klumpenhower

ISBN: 978-1-64507-188-4 (Print)
ISBN: 978-1-64507-189-1 (eBook)

Printed in the United States of America

28 27 26 25 24 23 22 21   1 2 3 4 5

God the protector of all that trust in Thee,
without whom nothing is strong, nothing is holy;
increase and multiply upon us Thy mercy;
that Thou being our ruler and guide,
we may so pass through things temporal, that we finally lose not
the things eternal: Grant this heavenly Father, for Jesus Christ's
sake our Lord. Amen.

The Collect, Fourth Sunday after Trinity,
The Book of Common Prayer

CONTENTS

INTRODUCTION

Many believers wonder why Ecclesiastes is even in the Bible. At first glance, it seems to offer little hope, which feels wrong for people who are trusting Jesus. But if you listen carefully to its wisdom, you will come to realize that its goal is to topple *false* hopes. Ecclesiastes wants to lead an insurrection in your heart. It will insist that you admit the wispy futility of your dreams for success, prosperity, pleasure, recognition, legacy, self-sufficiency, and even religious achievement. It will leave you with your hopes recalibrated. It will teach you to look at the life you have with new eyes and to look beyond this life and into eternity.

This means you can expect Ecclesiastes to make you more eager to know the Creator who put you in this often-frustrating world and more ready to practice his strange way of living in it. After all, your Creator has walked among us "under the sun," but did so with eternity's light as his guide. Just as you have no hope outside of him, you also have all hope in him. So, as with the other small-group resources in this series, this study guide will help you examine the Bible in a way that steers you toward this good news.

HOW TO USE THIS STUDY

This study guide will help you study Ecclesiastes within a group. Studying with others lets you benefit from what God is also teaching them, and it will give you encouragement and accountability as you struggle together with the hard themes found in this part of the Bible.

Like Ecclesiastes itself, this study guide assumes that every group member is caught up to some extent in the emptiness of this world and has a daily need to look beyond it. With this in mind, the group should be a place to be open about sins, frustrations, and the hard realities of life—even the Christian life. Don't expect every participant to be equally quick to see and accept what Ecclesiastes is teaching. Ecclesiastes is clear that life is difficult and that faith is a constant challenge rather than an easy fix. It invites you to ponder its claims rather than rubber-stamp them with a too-quick "amen."

Each participant should have one of these study guides in order to join in reading and be able to work through the exercises during that part of the study. *The study leader should read through both the lesson and the leader's notes in the back of this book before each lesson begins.* No other preparation or homework is required. A few sections of Ecclesiastes are skipped over in the group discussions, so some group members may want to read these on their own between group meetings, but it is not necessary to do so in order to fully participate in the discussions.

There are ten lessons in this study guide. Each lesson will take about an hour to complete, perhaps a bit more if your group is large, and will include these elements:

BIG IDEA. This is a summary of the main point of the lesson.

BIBLE CONVERSATION. You will read a passage from Ecclesiastes and discuss it. As the heading suggests, the Bible conversation questions are intended to spark a conversation rather than generate correct answers. In most cases, the questions will have several possible good answers and a few best answers. The leader's notes at the back of this book provide some insights, but don't just turn there for the "right answer." At times you may want to see what the notes say, but always try to answer for yourself first by thinking about the Bible passage.

ARTICLE. This is the main teaching section of the lesson, written by the book's author.

DISCUSSION. The discussion questions following the article will help you apply the teaching to your life.

EXERCISE. The exercise is a section you will complete on your own during group time. You can write in the book if that helps you. You will then share some of what you learned with the group. If the group is large, it may help to split up to share the results of the exercise and to pray, so that everyone has a better opportunity to participate.

WRAP-UP AND PRAYER. Prayer is a critical part of the lesson because your spiritual growth will happen through God's work in you, not by your self-effort. You will be asking him to do that good work.

Ecclesiastes specializes in disruption. Expect the Holy Spirit to use it to dismantle your time-bound idols. Ask him now to replace them with a deeper faith in Jesus that thrusts you, perhaps bewildered, into a life in light of eternity.

1

WISDOM

BIG IDEA

Godly wisdom begins with realizing that everything this world offers, including our lives here, is fleeting, unsatisfying, and without lasting impact—which leads us to abandon a "normal" way of living.

BIBLE CONVERSATION *20 MINUTES*

Ecclesiastes is a book of wisdom. This means it invites you to come to God more indirectly than you may be used to, by first pondering its sayings about life in the world. Traditionally, Ecclesiastes has been attributed to King Solomon since it mentions several biographical details that fit Israel's wisdom-seeking king. But the author, whoever he is, chooses to refer to himself anonymously as simply "the Preacher" or "the Teacher," and our study will follow his lead.

The Preacher beings with a summary statement: All is vanity (some translations say "meaningless" or "futility"). Since *vanity* can have many meanings, it's important to understand that here you should think of *vanity* in terms of "something that will vanish" or "something that is all in vain." The Hebrew word can mean "mist" or "breath," suggesting a vapor that will not last or is futile to try to grasp.

With this in mind, have someone read the Preacher's opening poem aloud from **Ecclesiastes 1:1–11**. Then discuss the questions below.

What is your initial reaction to the Preacher's opening statement that all things are a vanity of vanities? What have you seen in the world that might support this statement?

Read "between the lines" of the poem. List some of your deep longings it alludes to that are left unfulfilled in this world.

The Preacher observes that not only are we here and then gone, we leave no lasting impact anyone will remember for long. How might this thought change your approach to death?

****

Now read the article from this study guide's author. Take turns reading it aloud, switching readers at each paragraph break.

GET WISE

5 MINUTES

> Let a man meet a she-bear robbed of her cubs rather than
> a fool in his folly.
>
> Proverbs 17:12

A wild animal can tear you limb from limb, but the Bible says it is
nothing compared to the damage a fool can do.

Ecclesiastes, as part of the Bible's wisdom literature, is all about
how to get wise for life. It is one of God's beautiful gifts to us, but
it is a strange gift: it comes wrapped in riddles and conundrums.
Ecclesiastes requires that we brace ourselves and learn to look
at the world from a very different angle. Folly looks at the world
normally, but wisdom gives us an unusual lens.

This is the gospel way. It turns things upside down, and inside
out, and back to front. The first will be last, the least will be the
greatest, and the way to find your life is to lose it.

A BOOK WITH A SURPRISING GIFT

On September 15, 2001, the former Formula One race car driver
Alex Zanardi was involved in a terrible crash which required

him to have both legs amputated. Fifteen years later, at the Rio Paralympics, Zanardi won gold in the handcycling event. On receiving his medal, Zanardi said, "I feel my life is a never-ending privilege. . . . Even my accident, what happened to me, became the greatest opportunity of my life."[1] I sit up and take notice when I hear someone like Zanardi speak. There is always something beautiful—and disorientating—in finding a gift where we only thought to find tragedy.

In these studies, I want to suggest that God intends Ecclesiastes to have the same jolting effect in our lives. Zanardi's words echo the worldview of the author of Ecclesiastes. Many have been baffled by his repeated refrain, "Vanity of vanities! All is vanity," and by the jarring ways this part of God's Word seems to speak about life in his world. But the brilliance of Ecclesiastes is to unearth gifts in that most awful, most strange, and most bitter place of all: death.

The biggest adjustment we have to make in reading Ecclesiastes is grasping what the Teacher is doing with the reality of our own coming death. He does not say death is a good thing. He does not deny it is a shattering curse; in fact, that reality courses through all he says. But he does believe that is not all there is to say about death. The tragic fact that one day I will be no more and be forgotten by the generations who follow can be, in Zanardi-like words, an invitation to the greatest opportunity of my life. If we really believe that we will die, and accept that coming reality, then we can learn how to live.

A WORD WITH A STARTLING MEANING

The Teacher makes this point in many ways. His argument is not linear and logical, but more like an artist layering a canvas with different textures. One of his brush strokes appears already in the second verse of the book: "Vanity of vanities, says the Preacher;

vanity of vanities! All is vanity." The word *vanity* translates the Hebrew word *hebel* which some have rendered as "meaningless." Such a reading poses many problems for us as we grapple with how life in God's world could possibly be meaningless.

But a better translation of *hebel* is "mist" or "vapor." In Psalm 39:4–5, David asks God to teach him the measure of his days and to let him know how fleeting he is. We often speak of time as fleeting, but David says that *he* is fleeting: "Surely all mankind stands as a mere breath [*hebel*]!" In Psalm 144:4, David says again, "Man is like a breath [*hebel*]; his days are like a passing shadow."

So the idea with this word *hebel* is not that life is pointless, an existential dead end devoid of purpose and meaning. Rather, almost everything about life—and especially our lives as human creatures in the world—has a morning mist-like quality. We come with an expiration date, and so do most other things. When you set human lives in the context of world history, stretching back behind us and rolling on past us, we are no more long-lasting than the dew on your lawn this morning. The Preacher wants you to make a coffee and sit down and think really hard about what that means for your life.

A QUESTION WITH A SHOCKING ANSWER

To help this startling word *hebel* percolate into your system, the Preacher asks a stark question in the very next verse: "What does man gain by all the toil at which he toils under the sun?" The whole of Ecclesiastes is the Preacher's own answer to this question, but his answer is a shock: Nothing. Or, at very best, not much.

The word *gain* here carries the idea of a surplus, something left over, a life that finishes in the black not the red. He's referring to the innate desire we all have in one way or another to leave a legacy with our life, and for what we do to have a lasting significance beyond all the effort and toil we pour into our lives.

It's important to keep reading Ecclesiastes over and over until you can tune into this Preacher's unusual message. He is not saying that toil and effort and industry are worthless; on the contrary, he sees them as good gifts (see Ecclesiastes 9:9–10). Rather, right at the start of his long sermon, the Preacher is here flagging up something he knows to be true of every sinful human being this side of the fall: we want too much for ourselves from our labors.

The writer of Ecclesiastes, in his unique and inspired way, has seen into the human heart and observed the particular form of pride that first lurked in Eden and still resides in us all. We want to be like God by knowing it all and having it all, and we want to build our own towers to reach to the skies. If we think about death at all, it is something that happens to other people. For ourselves, we think we will live, we will work, we will achieve, we will go here and there and do this or that with our lives. And then we hear God speaking to us, through the words of this strange Preacher, that death comes to us all and the world has already long forgotten the people who came behind us and will soon forget the people who come after us.

Learning to hear this message as a gift might mean we have to unlearn some "normal" ways we think about life. But receiving Ecclesiastes as the sharp goad of a loving Shepherd (Ecclesiastes 12:11) is to embrace a wonderfully wise path to life.

DISCUSSION *10 MINUTES*

What kind of legacy have you hoped to leave when your life here is over, and what "toils" have you worked at to try to make it happen?

At this point, do you feel you need to hear the jolting words of the Preacher? Explain.

Lesson

EXERCISE

THE UPSIDE-DOWN LIFE

20 MINUTES

Life's normal responses to the vanity described in Ecclesiastes might include striving anyway, giving up, denial, or escaping into amusements. But as the article mentioned, the gospel teaches us to look at life in a new, unusual way that "turns things upside down, and inside out, and back to front."

Jesus went through life that way. Although he is God, he "did not count equality with God a thing to be grasped, but emptied himself, by taking the form of a servant" (Philippians 2:6–7). When we stop grasping for the mist, we not only learn from Jesus but walk alongside him and enjoy his gifts.

This exercise introduces some ways the gospel life is not normal. Begin by completing the exercise on your own. Read through the descriptions of life with Jesus, and then answer the questions at the end. You'll finish by sharing some of your responses with the group.

1. The way up is down. Sharing in Christ brings the relief of letting go of your urge to get ahead. It changes the meaning of greatness.

It means sharing Jesus's life of service to others and surrender to God, trusting him to lift you up in due time.

> "Whoever would be great among you must be your servant, and whoever would be first among you must be slave of all. For even the Son of Man came not to be served but to serve, and to give his life as a ransom for many." (Mark 10:43–45)

2. The path to life leads through death. The sweetest fellowship comes when you die daily to your dreams of success, your self-reliance, and your need for worldly rewards and recognition—and finally when your body itself dies and you enter Christ's presence and then join in his resurrection.

> "Unless a grain of wheat falls into the earth and dies, it remains alone; but if it dies, it bears much fruit. Whoever loves his life loses it, and whoever hates his life in this world will keep it for eternal life." (John 12:24–25)

3. You must see what can't be seen. Though your body is wasting away and your worldly dreams are a mist, Jesus is preparing for you an eternal, weighty, lasting glory.

> We look not to the things that are seen but to the things that are unseen. For the things that are seen are transient, but the things that are unseen are eternal. (2 Corinthians 4:18)

4. True wisdom looks like foolishness. The message that Jesus died for you sounds like foolishness that only weak, lowly, and despised people might accept. But if you believe it, God saves you through it.

> Has not God made foolish the wisdom of the world? (1 Corinthians 1:20)

5. When you are weak, you are strong. Your very inability to take hold of what you want or even to serve God makes you rely more on him, the source of true strength.

> I will boast all the more gladly of my weaknesses, so that the power of Christ may rest upon me. (2 Corinthians 12:9)

6. Growth comes by God's power, not willpower. It's hard to take the low place, die to self, welcome weakness, and live for what is unseen. Striving to achieve such a life for yourself is just as futile as any other self-focused striving. Instead, you receive this life from God, as a gift, as you draw near to him daily.

> "Whoever abides in me and I in him, he it is that bears much fruit, for apart from me you can do nothing." (John 15:5)

Which description of the gospel's unusual way to live feels hardest to you? If you can, explain why._____

_____

_____

Which description fits a way you have already noticed God working in you. Note how._____

_____

_____

Which Bible passage above, taken along with Ecclesiastes 1:1–11, most encourages you to know Jesus better. Why?_____

_____

_____

When the group is ready, share some of your responses.

WRAP-UP AND PRAYER *10 MINUTES*

Of course, other parts of the Bible teach us that in Christ we do have both lasting impact and newness: "In the Lord your labor is not in vain" (1 Corinthians 15:58), and "Behold, I am making all things new" (Revelation 21:5). But the Preacher in Ecclesiastes is not so clumsy as to tell us this up front. He will make us ponder and squirm and struggle with the world first. This will be the focus of our next few lessons.

You might use your closing prayer time together to pray for the coming lessons in this study, asking God to use the sharp words of Ecclesiastes to prick you in helpful ways.

2

HAPPINESS

BIG IDEA

The more we try to find lasting satisfaction in the many offerings of happiness in this world, the more we find we instead need to look somewhere else entirely.

BIBLE CONVERSATION *20 MINUTES*

In the opening chapters of his treatise, the Preacher explores the human desire for happiness and the huge variety of ways we pursue this, from pleasure to industry, architecture, horticulture, work, and education. He leaves virtually no stone unturned. Still he finds that all they promise is vanity—fleeting and impossible to catch, like a mist.

Have several readers take turns reading **Ecclesiastes 1:12–2:26** aloud. Then discuss the questions below.

In chapter 1 and in verses 12–17 of chapter 2, the Preacher affirms that wise living is better than being foolish, but insists that even wisdom ends in vanity. Which of his comments about the vanity of a sensible life strike you as especially true, and why?

Verses 1–11 of chapter 2 are about indulging in pleasures, acquiring possessions, and achieving success. Which of the Preacher's examples remind you of happiness strategies you've tried? Explain.

Verses 18–26 of chapter 2 are about hard work going for nothing. What parts can you relate to, and why?

****

Now think more about the search for happiness by reading this lesson's article. Take turns reading it aloud, switching readers at each paragraph break.

ARTICLE

HOW TO BE HAPPY

5 MINUTES

Creatures are not born with desires unless satisfaction for those desires exists. A baby feels hunger: well, there is such a thing as food. A duckling wants to swim: well, there is such a thing as water. Men feel sexual desire: well, there is such a thing as sex. If I find in myself a desire which no experience in this world can satisfy, the most probable explanation is that I was made for another world. If none of my earthly pleasures satisfy it, that does not prove that the universe is a fraud. Probably earthly pleasures were never meant to satisfy it, but only to arouse it, to suggest the real thing. If that is so, I must take care, on the one hand, never to despise, or be unthankful for, these earthly blessings, and on the other, never to mistake them for the something else of which they are only a kind of copy, or echo, or mirage. I must keep alive in myself the desire for my true country, which I shall not find until after death.

C. S. Lewis, *Mere Christianity*

If you've ever wondered how to do what C. S. Lewis says we must do—keep alive the innate desire for our true heavenly country—then Ecclesiastes is here to help. The Preacher knows that all our earthly desires can so easily drown our longing for the real thing. So he sets about showing us how not to get lost in our longings.

In examining the places we look for pleasure, the Preacher already knows what Blaise Pascal came to know many centuries later: "All men seek happiness. This is without exception. Whatever different means they use, they all tend to this end. The cause of some going to war, and of others avoiding it, is the same desire in both—to be happy. This is the motive of every action of every man."[2]

And yet this faithful Israelite Preacher, who knows the God of the law and the covenants with his people, also knows other things about life which inform what he learns about happiness.

LIFE IS ALWAYS SHORT

The Preacher is not just seeking pleasure; he is using it to explore both wisdom and folly "till I might see what was good for the children of man to do under heaven during the few days of their life" (2:3). One aspect of the *hebel* ("vanity") nature of life is that, like dew on a lawn, or your breath in a frosty morning or on a cold mirror, so too the life we've been given is short. We are here one minute but gone the next. As strange as it might be, it actually takes wisdom to know this, for we spend a lot of our lives assuming we will live forever. When we are young, we think old age will never come to us; when we are old, we can't believe how quickly we lost our youth. The older we get the more we find ourselves having to face the fact that the days of our life are few.

LIFE IS USUALLY ELUSIVE

The Preacher discovers not just that life is short, but that what it seems to offer also eludes your grasp. Life comes and goes, leaving you wondering how to hold on to the things that really seemed to make it worth living. Someone has said that we do not know that we are happy, only that we were. If you try to put happiness in a safe, or frame it or bottle it, you just can't do it. Life is like smoke from a candle or wind rustling through the trees. You simply can't put it in your pocket and keep it forever.

Happiness doesn't last when you get to it, because when you find the thing you've been working for and longing for—when you actually have it in your hands—you discover it's not everything you hoped it would be. "Then I considered all that my hands had done and the toil I had expended in doing it, and behold, all was vanity and a striving after wind" (2:11). Some psychologists talk about the *progress principle*. They say there's a universal principle at work in the human heart and mind, which is that we find more pleasure in working toward a goal than we experience when we actually attain it. You will certainly have tasted something of this for yourself.

LIFE IS OFTEN UNJUST

But it's not just that happiness doesn't last because of life's brevity and life's elusiveness. It also doesn't last because we cannot control its presence in the future. We have no control of what will become of the work of our hands. "I hated all my toil in which I toil under the sun, seeing that I must leave it to the man who will come after me, and who knows whether he will be wise, or a fool? Yet he will be master of all for which I toiled and used my wisdom under the sun. This also is vanity" (2:18–19).

How do we find lasting happiness and deep peace and satisfaction in the world when we realize that it all slips from our fingers and one day will leave us forever when we die? The same fate overtakes both the wise and the fool, both believers and unbelievers. Even living wisely won't stop us being present at our own funerals one day, exactly the same as the town fool who lives down the street. We all die, and our lives are so short and what we achieve doesn't seem to last. So where is the happiness in living with that knowledge?

So far, the only real chink of light the Preacher has given us is his repeated use of the phrase "under the sun." In the ancient world the sun marked time, not space. The days under the sun refer to these days of temporal existence, the whole of human history from the beginning of time until the end of time. These are the days "under the sun." In these days, we are often left with many questions and few answers. We wrestle with immense perplexity on a global scale and in the minutiae of our lives.

But these time-bound days of brief human existence are not the only kind of days there will be. On the other side of time is God and eternity.

DISCUSSION *10 minutes*

What has been your approach to the increasing realization that life is short and desires go unmet? Do you think it's a healthy approach? Why or why not?

How are the vanities of life, experienced by both believers and unbelievers, a good way for you to connect with people who don't yet know Jesus? Explain how you might make those connections.

Lesson

EXERCISE

WHAT'S IN YOUR BARNS?

20 MINUTES

Jesus may have had Ecclesiastes in mind when he told his Parable of the Rich Fool. In that story, a man had so many possessions that his barns could not hold them, so he decided to build larger barns. Jesus said the rich man thought to himself, "'I will say to my soul, Soul, you have ample goods laid up for many years; relax, eat, drink, be merry.' But God said to him, 'Fool! This night your soul is required of you, and the things you have prepared, whose will they be?' So is the one who lays up treasure for himself and is not rich toward God" (Luke 12:19–21).

For this exercise, think about what "barns" you tend to build. Be honest: What earthly treasures do you try to store up for yourself? Work through the exercise on your own. You'll have a chance to share when you're done.

PART 1: Note some of the "barns" you are most likely to build for yourself.

❏ **Barns full of SECURITY.** I work to surround myself with things and people that make me feel safe and lessen my sense of worry.

21

❐ **Barns full of COMFORT.** "Relax, eat, drink, and be merry" sounds good to me. I seek out the money, people, and living situations that make it possible.

❐ **Barns full of WISDOM and KNOWLEDGE.** I trust my smarts, my education, my experience, or my sound theology to help me be an achiever.

❐ **Barns full of GOOD BEHAVIOR.** I trust in sensible life decisions to make things work out for me, or in pious habits to earn blessings from God.

❐ **Barns full of PLEASURES.** I try to amass fun experiences or attain a preferred lifestyle that lets me enjoy my days.

❐ **Barns full of ACCOMPLISHMENTS.** If I can look back at what I have done and feel good about it, I will be satisfied.

❐ **Barns full of HARD WORK.** I pride myself in doing my best and keeping at it. Good things are bound to come from that.

❐ **Barns full of LEGACY.** My goal is to leave something of value in this world or be remembered, or to have my ideals and strengths live on in my family, church, workplace, or other community.

❐ **Barns full of APPROVAL.** I want people to admire me for my work, my family, my abilities, my godly living, or my successes, or I want them to like me for my personality, lifestyle, virtues, or other traits.

❐ **Barns full of** _____. (Pick your own that's true of you.)

PART 2: Jesus followed his parable with teaching that points out some of the gifts God gives believers—gifts that help us let go of our barns. Read these excerpts from his teaching, and note or underline a part you find especially helpful.

Gift #1: Fatherly care. Jesus said, "Do not be anxious about your life, what you will eat, nor about your body, what you will put on. For life is more than food, and the body more than clothing. . . . For all the nations of the world seek after these things, and your Father knows that you need them" (Luke 12:22–23, 30). You have a loving Father who sees to all your needs. Trusting in things of this world leads to anxiety, but letting go of them leads you to trust your Father.

Gift #2: God's kingdom. Jesus said, "Fear not, little flock, for it is your Father's good pleasure to give you the kingdom" (Luke 12:32). You have a tender Shepherd who brings you into his fold and calls you to share in his mission—caring for others and telling about Jesus. You *can* have an impact that lasts if you work for the kingdom that lasts.

Gift #3: A treasure in heaven. Jesus said, "Sell your possessions, and give to the needy. Provide yourselves with moneybags that do not grow old, with a treasure in the heavens that does not fail" (Luke 12:33). Your most precious heavenly treasure, lasting and unfailing, is Jesus himself. You are freed up to give to others because Jesus, not your possessions, gives the happiness you long for: "In your presence there is fullness of joy; at your right hand are pleasures forevermore" (Psalm 16:11).

When the group is ready, share some of your responses. If you can, try to explain *why* you build certain "barns." How might the wisdom of Ecclesiastes or the gifts Jesus mentioned help you let those barns go?

WRAP-UP AND PRAYER *10 MINUTES*

You might want to pray together that your Father would help you let go of things that are vanity and hold onto the promises of your Savior.

3

TIME

BIG IDEA

Our time in this world comes with rhythms and seasons of life that we wish to control but must learn to accept as coming from God, who controls time.

BIBLE CONVERSATION *20 MINUTES*

As you approach Ecclesiastes 3, it will help to keep in mind two connected truths found in verse 11. The first is that God "has made everything beautiful in its time." He controls the rhythms and seasons of our lives, and his plans are perfect. But the second is that, despite giving us hearts that sense these eternal plans and long to see how they come together, we "cannot find out what God has done from beginning to end."

With this in mind, have someone read **Ecclesiastes 3** aloud, or have several participants take turns. Then discuss the questions below.

Consider the list of happenings and chores that each have their time. Would you, like the Teacher, call them all "beautiful"? What other labels might you give them, and why?

In verses 9–15, the Teacher lays out his response to the frustration of not being able to find out God's eternal plans. What do you like, or not like, about his response? Explain.

Verses 16–22 remind us that it's hard to see how evil will be made right or how our deaths are any different than the death of an animal. Have you ever thought some of the things the Teacher dares to say here? Explain.

****

Now take turns reading aloud the article from this study guide's author, switching readers with each paragraph. Then discuss the questions that follow.

Lesson

ARTICLE

MY TIMES ARE IN HIS HANDS

5 MINUTES

The great evangelist Billy Graham died on February 21, 2018. In the weeks after his death, I watched many video clips of his worldwide ministry, and one in particular has stuck with me. Preaching in Southern Seminary Chapel in 1982, Graham said that at age sixty-four his greatest surprise in life was the brevity of life: "If someone had told me when I was twenty years old that life was very short and would pass—just like that—I wouldn't have believed it. And if I tell you that, you don't believe it either. I cannot get young people to understand how brief life is, how quickly it passes."[3]

Time. Flying past us. Not enough of it. Slipping away from us. Always pressed for it. Wishing we were better at managing it. Feeling guilty we don't have more for someone special, or something noble. We are always running out of time. And Billy Graham is right—oh, how quickly it passes.

Time is a profoundly theological entity. A timeless God teaches creatures some of his greatest lessons in the vehicle of time. It has both a linear and a circular form—you can't repeat time, even as it gifts you many things on a repeating loop. All of it educates us about what God loves and about what it means to be human.

THE PATH OF WISDOM RESPECTS TIME'S RHYTHMS

"For everything there is a season, and a time for every matter under heaven." It's worth pausing right there, at the entrance to this most famous of reflections on time.

Scripture says there is a time for all things, but our world counters that—instead, all things can be done all the time. Most technology, for instance, has harnessed us to the lie that we can throw off the creaturely restraints of time and have access to everything always, without waiting, without stopping, and without needing to rest. Electricity blurs the boundaries between working while it is day and sleeping while it is night, and our online life has become our timeless master, as several screens ping commands without end which we obey without question. Gyms, fuel stations, libraries, offices, and supermarkets are open 24/7, and we come to believe we can do everything all the time. There is no particular season for anything. We do what we want, when we want.

But wise people respect time's rhythms. Dawn, morning, after-noon, evening, night. God made six days to work, one day to rest. This structures a week, which repeats over a month, and the months in years. Many people try to live rhythm-free lives by simply doing whatever they feel like doing in any given moment, without proper attention to whether it is the right time to do that thing; this actually tears at the fabric of what it means to be human. We are now discovering that our constant, seasonless attention to digital media is diminishing our personhood. In years of pastoral ministry, I have not seen many families unravel who observe the Lord's Day together in unbroken rhythm, with deliberate joy and routine hospitality. But I do see others whose devotion to the church body is constantly interrupted by this or that, and it is a symptom of an unruly, irregular rhythm that doesn't promote peace and rest.

THE PATH OF FOLLY SEEKS TO CONTROL TIME'S SEASONS

Rhythms are not all there is in an ordinary life under the sun. There is also "a time to be born, and a time to die." There is "a time to weep, and a time to laugh." There is "a time to love, and a time to hate." These are seasons we find ourselves in, not rhythms we regularly repeat. There is no predictability to their appearance in our timelines and often their presence takes us by surprise. It requires the eye of faith to see that God "has made everything beautiful in its time," because we often live with life's ugliness and pain as much as its beauty and delight. Further, these are relational seasons: they involve people we love and lose, those we wrong and forgive, those we befriend and those who do us harm. We are profoundly relational beings, and most of our lives are taken up with navigating the different seasons of our relationships and the effects they have on us.

Such seasons expose how little control we actually have over our lives. Zack Eswine says, "Many of our frustrations rise from our blindness to the change of season or to the pain or joy of them, and we struggle to adjust our expectations."[4] What do we do with those seasons which bring wrecking-ball damage to our tidy little realms? Where do we turn?

Ecclesiastes helps us to see that one of the seasons we do not control is the time for justice: "I said in my heart, God will judge the righteous and the wicked, for there is a time for every matter and every work" (v. 17). There will be a time, one day, for divine time travel: "God seeks what has been driven away" (v. 15). All the events of human history that have slipped through the hourglass of time into the past might be lost to us—but they are never lost to God. One day, he will dial back time and fetch the past into his present to bring it to account. Each and every time will have its day in court.

Foolish people seek all the answers to life in each and every season of life. But some seasons yield only questions, not answers. Some seasons bring a wound that will not heal; it might take a lifetime to learn that we "cannot find out what God has done from the beginning to the end." The story of my life has broken characters, jarring interruptions, unexpected joys, and relationships caught up in unresolved tensions and difficulties. In God's kindness I have, as yet, unfinished chapters. But my story is not *the* story. "*The* story reveals that there will be a time of judgment, and believers trust that judgment will finally prevail."[5]

THE PATH OF LIFE EMBRACES TIME'S REVERSALS

This perspective is the gospel's now-and-not-yet voice speaking in the unfamiliar accent of Ecclesiastes. It is life in the light of eternity. Today is the time of suffering and anguish, of work and pleasure, of toil and terror; tomorrow is the time of glory and judgment, of the resurrection of the body and life everlasting in a world without end.

Now this, tomorrow that. The Lord Jesus fills our time with the unspeakable comfort of promised great reversals. Lose your life today for the sake of Jesus and his gospel; save it tomorrow. Gain the world now; forfeit your soul then. Be ashamed of Jesus in the time of this sinful generation; witness him being ashamed of you in the time of his coming in the glory of the Father and the holy angels.*

Believers on the road to life know that the experiences of time can be reversed. The gospel turns the world on its head. Marred beyond human resemblance, the Servant of the Lord comes, in time, to shut the mouths of kings. Buried with the wicked, he comes, in time, to divide the spoils of the strong.** Blessed are those who are poor in spirit, who mourn, who are meek, who are hungry, those who lose everything in the here and now—for the day of reversal is coming and the reward will be great in the kingdom of heaven.***

DISCUSSION *10 MINUTES*

Which path do you walk most often: (1) the wisdom path of respect for rhythms, (2) the folly path of trying to control time, or (3) the life path of hope in God's reversals?

What events in your life do you most try to control? What would change if you remembered that God controls them?

---

* Mark 8:35–38
** Isaiah 53:12
*** Matthew 5:2–12

Lesson

EXERCISE

3

FIXING OR FAITH

20 MINUTES

Pondering the times in our lives will bring us either to frustration from trying to fix them or to faith. God first lets us discover the vanities of our time-bound lives so that we turn to him. Only he has control over all things, even time.

For this exercise, consider where you are on the path from fixing to faith. (NOTE: Responding to circumstances in your life by trying to fix or control them is a natural reaction for fallen people. We all want to minimize pain and hold on to things that make us happy. But Ecclesiastes reminds us that God uses all the seasons of life to show us our need for him. Even when we are frustrated by bad things, God is helping us see that we can truly rely only on him. His blessings last because they come to us through faith in Jesus. So don't be afraid to see where you act like a fixer. Seeing the true depth of your need can show you how to come to Christ as your only source of comfort and stability.)

Work through the exercise on your own. You'll first consider happenings that are hard times. Note whether you tend to respond by FIXING, in FAITH, or somewhere in between. Then do the same for good times, noting your tendency for CONTROL or FAITH.

When the group is ready, discuss the questions at the end of the exercise.

In HARD Times

FIXING

I must take control. I try to end hard times or soften their hurt by withdrawing, assigning blame, or doggedly trying to repair what is happening now.

FAITH

My God is in control. In his time, he will use, overcome, and one day reverse what is happening now.

When I face death (my own, or the death of others), I respond with . . .

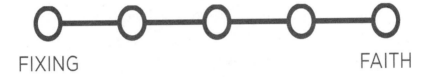

FIXING   FAITH

When I feel the loss of a special person, place, experience, or time in life, I respond with . . .

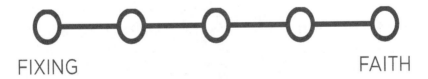

FIXING   FAITH

When the world's injustices and problems feel overwhelming, I respond with . . .

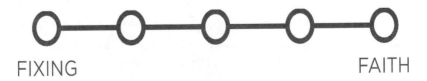

FIXING   FAITH

When others sin in ways that make me angry, I respond with . . .

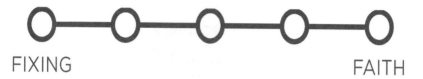

FIXING   FAITH

When I sin and feel its guilt or its consequences, I respond with . . .

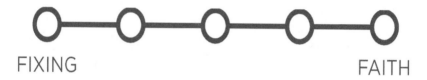

FIXING   FAITH

When my success is not as satisfying as I hoped it would be, I respond with . . .

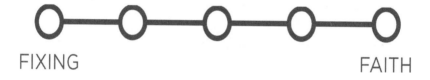

FIXING   FAITH

In GOOD Times

CONTROL	FAITH
I am desperate to make this last. I must manage it and keep it and fix the fact that it might slip away.	My God rules time. I take these good times as a temporary gift from him and a preview of the lasting pleasures he has in store for me in the next life.

When things are going well for my family and other loved ones, I respond with . . .

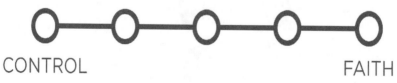

CONTROL   FAITH

When things are going well with my work or career, I respond with . . .

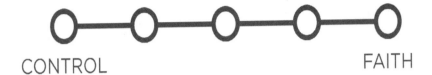

CONTROL   FAITH

When things are going well for the church, I respond with . . .

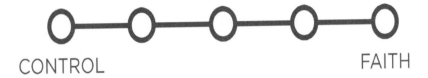

CONTROL   FAITH

When things are going well in the world and politics, I respond with . . .

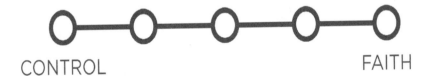

CONTROL   FAITH

When things are going well for my relationships, I respond with . . .

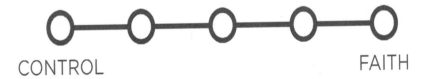

CONTROL   FAITH

When things are going well health-wise, I respond with . . .

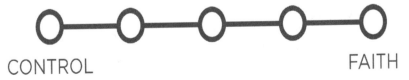

CONTROL   FAITH

Now share some of your responses with the group. What patterns do you notice? What specific behaviors in your life are evidence of attempts at fixing and control, or of faith? What has God been teaching you?

WRAP-UP AND PRAYER *10 MINUTES*

You might close by praying about some problems that seem unfixable in this world, asking God to work both within and outside the bounds of time to make things right and be good to you, his child. Ask him also to give you faith to believe in things unseen and eternal.

4

JUSTICE

BIG IDEA

The world is full of persistent injustice, but Jesus brings a fuller answer to oppression than the world can offer.

BIBLE CONVERSATION *20 MINUTES*

Ecclesiastes 3 ended with an encouragement to rejoice in our work, but chapter 4 raises some concerns. Our work too often is done under oppression. Or it is done out of envy, or tainted with laziness, or awash in loneliness, or lacking support from others. Have someone read **Ecclesiastes 4** aloud. Then discuss the questions below.

Verses 1–3 are brutally bleak about oppression in the world. Is injustice really that bad and unfixable? Explain.

Compare what this passage says about acting alone (not heeding advice, acting out of envy) versus working together. What insights do you appreciate, and why?

How might the wisdom about working together and for each other be an answer to the problem of oppression? Is it a good enough answer?

NOTE: The rest of the Bible gives an answer to the question of whether or not injustice is fixable. Once you have finished your Bible conversation, it would be good, in this case, for you to turn to the lesson 4 leader's notes in the back of this study guide and compare your responses to the comments there.

****

Now take turns reading through the article aloud, switching readers at each paragraph break. When you finish, discuss the questions that follow.

Lesson

ARTICLE

STOP THE INJUSTICE

5 MINUTES

One of the things I find most compelling about Christianity is that the more I taste of life's hard edges and brutality, the more I discover the Bible got there before me. It is not a world of fairy tales and make-believe. The Christian faith encourages us to use our eyes to look at the world the way it really is and to face head-on the facts of what we see around us. It invites hard thought, not escapism.

You might have to read the opening words of Ecclesiastes 4 a few times to check that something like this really is in the Bible. But our Preacher takes seriously the world as it is really is. Although these words were written thousands of years ago, they have continued to describe every generation of humanity right through to our present time. Black lives and the legacy of slavery. Starving children. Human trafficking and sexual abuse in all its degrading forms. There are some sufferings and injustices that are so indescribably bleak the only real response is to weep. I have my personal experiences of injustice, and you will have yours, and we carry these weights with us wherever we go.

What does a life wisely lived look like in the face of all this? The first thing to remember is that Ecclesiastes is painting a richly textured picture, not giving simple one-word answers. The picture emerging is, in fact, that only the Christian faith has a deeply satisfying answer to injustice. But to develop this portrait, the Preacher takes his time. He has what I call a "depth" view to the problem of injustice, and also a "long" view. We'll come to the long view in our final study, but for now let's think about his depth answer.

In essence it's this: the Christian faith says you never solve injustice without changing the heart of the oppressor, the one doing the damage. The Bible describes that damage and paints a picture of it that is compelling and real. No one ever talks about the internal dynamics of the oppressor and what's happening to them as they damage others. We all focus on the victim, and rightly so in many ways. They've had something awful done to them and they need both justice and healing for the wrongs they have borne. But what are the oppressors doing to themselves?

We will never solve the problem of injustice unless we change the hearts of people who oppress, and the Christian faith knows this and has something to say about it: "Then I saw that all toil and all skill in work come from a man's envy of his neighbor. This also is vanity and a striving after wind" (v. 4). Ecclesiastes looks beneath the surface and sees an evil like envy wrapping its tentacles around the human heart and says that the reason you are oppressing your neighbor is because you have not realized that God made you to love your neighbor and to give to your neighbor, not take from your neighbor.

Martin Luther King Jr. had a dream. He dreamed of the day when people would not be judged by the color of their skin but by the content of their character. Yet this just gives us another level of problem: What *is* the content of our character? What are we really like on the inside? If I were to judge you by your character—and by that, I mean if I were to judge you by what *you* know is really true about you—what would I think of you? And what would you think of me if you knew all there is to know about me? Don't we need something to change our character? Doesn't the problem of injustice "out there" in the world start with "in here" in the human heart—and who can really do anything about that?

God can do something about it. God can change us from the inside out. This is the deep reason why the Christian faith has an answer to injustice you won't find anywhere else. Forget school reform and better education and improved social welfare and healthcare as ends in themselves. Unless people are made new from the inside out, nothing really changes in a truly lasting way.

It is right, of course, that we seek to live and act justly, that we love righteousness and that we show mercy. This honors Christ. It lets our light shine before others, so that they may see our good works and give glory to our Father in heaven.* I want to be very clear that to ignore these things strikes against our very identity as believers.

But the Lord Jesus is also clear that the heart of the human problem is the human heart.** It's why today's radical movement for change and liberation soon becomes tomorrow's outdated monument to human stubbornness and pride unless the good news of forgiveness of sin and the promise of a new heart is front and center. In this way, when followers of Christ preach the gospel and work out its implications for righteousness, truth, and justice, we foreshadow the great day of judgment that Ecclesiastes so clearly asks us to pin our hopes on.

The gospel light that is beginning to break in the pages of Ecclesiastes at this point flows from its deep conviction that the wise path to life is found in covenantal obedience to the law of God: "Two are better than one, because they have a better reward for their

---

* Matthew 5:16
** Mark 7:14–23

toil." Don't rush past the verses about two working together to help each other. The Teacher in Ecclesiastes might have a strange accent, and we have to listen hard to catch it, but in fact he has the same voice as the Lord Jesus Christ who said that the first and second most important commandments were these: "You shall love the Lord your God with all your heart and with all your soul and with all your mind and with all your strength" and, "You shall love your neighbor as yourself" (Mark 12:30, 31).

Together, our Old Testament Teacher and our ultimate Teacher, the Lord Jesus, tell us that we must be rescued from loving and serving ourselves to a life of loving and serving God and others. Until then, we will always carry inside us the seeds of injustice that can destroy us from the inside out and devastate the world in the process.

DISCUSSION *15 MINUTES*

What injustices are you are rightly angry about that have been done to you or others?

What part of Jesus's answer to injustice, including how he might involve you, most encourages you?

What has been your experience with "seeds of injustice" inside of you? How has God helped you to repent and love others?

EXERCISE

RESPONDING TO INJUSTICE

20 MINUTES

We are right to get angry at injustice and also to work to end it. But by now, Ecclesiastes has also taught us that our efforts alone, if disconnected from Jesus, won't accomplish much that lasts. Instead, we must work for justice as servants of Jesus, the Judge who brings perfect justice:

- Justice that is not only external, but reaches the heart
- Justice that is not only among our fellow humans in this world, but extends to our life with God
- Justice that not only frees the oppressed, but also the oppressor
- Justice that is not only for now, but will be perfect and lasting in the life to come

When we realize this, we will respond to injustice in a gospel-centered way rather than a worldly way.

Begin this exercise on your own by reading the descriptions of some worldly and gospel ways we might respond to injustice.

They begin with how we respond to the fact that we ourselves have been unjust (which is one important truth the gospel tells us) and move to how we respond to injustice done by others. Note a few pairs that especially apply to you, challenge you, or otherwise feel meaningful. When the group is ready, discuss the questions at the end of the exercise.

WORLDLY Response to Injustice	GOSPEL Response to Injustice
Blaming. My first concern is the wrong ways some people treat others and/or me.	**Self-awareness.** My first concern is the wrong ways I treat others and, most of all, God.
Hiding. When it comes to *my* wrongdoing, my instinct is to deny it, make excuses, shift blame, or hope God is lenient—though I still feel guilty.	**Hidden in Christ.** I have no need to hide or feel guilty, since Jesus covers my wrongdoing. The greatest act to deal with injustice came at the cross—done for me, the guilty party! This frees me to be honest about how I've hurt others.
Self-improvement. I hope to make myself into someone who treats others better, if I can.	**Growth in Christ.** God works in me to make me repentant in my heart—truly ready to love him and others. I know he can do it.
Progress. I must do my small part to live in a way that is more just. It's all I can do.	**Completion.** God not only is working to make me more just now, but one day will finish his work in me. He will make me completely fit to live in his remade world of perfect justice.
Making an effort. Changing myself into a person of justice is done by awareness and self-effort.	**Receiving grace.** I can't make myself into a person of justice, but God can. My first duty is to remain near to him and receive renewal from him. That's how I become more loving.
Retribution. When *others* have done wrong, someone must pay! The world needs justice.	**Right-making.** There's no doubt: either Jesus will make the guilty pay, or he has paid the price himself if they turn to him. To get full justice, the world needs Jesus.

WORLDLY Response to Injustice	GOSPEL Response to Injustice
Bitterness. I nurse grudges and constantly look for something new to be angry about.	**Hope.** Along with being rightly angry at injustice, I constantly look for Jesus to bring healing and forgiveness—and to use me in the process.
Judging. My anger at injustice is a way to feel good about myself. I'm on the right side!	**Gentleness.** My anger at injustice is tempered by humility and compassion. I remain ready to forgive as God in Christ has forgiven me.
External change. I hope that changing the structures and institutions of society will be enough to end injustice.	**Internal change.** My hope is in Jesus, who alone can do even more and also change people on the inside, in their hearts.
Justice as an idol. I serve the cause of justice! I hope some of what I accomplish will last.	**Justice as mission.** I serve Christ and his kingdom as it breaks into our present world. I'm all the more determined to pursue justice because kingdom work for justice *will* last; it is a taste of the final restoration Jesus will bring.
Impatience. I swing from hopelessness to demandingness. The world needs to get better, and it isn't happening fast enough.	**Patience.** I'm passionate about justice, but I know there will always be much "striving after wind" in this world. This means I am also able to rest. In time, Jesus will bring full justice.
We can do it. Making the world a more just place is accomplished by right thinking, hard work, or diligent activism.	**He can do it.** Only Jesus can bring the world justice that lasts. So my work and witness must always be accompanied by prayer.

Share your results with the group. Which items caught your attention, and why?

Sometimes we are dismissive about injustice either because we fail to see the beauty of godly justice or because we are rightly bothered by worldly approaches to justice. How might a gospel approach make you less dismissive, and instead eager to fight injustice?

WRAP-UP AND PRAYER *10 MINUTES*

Practice faith that Jesus can end injustice by praying for it. You might mention specific injustices you know about, including your own sinful advantage-taking. Pray for God to change hearts, for his kingdom to keep breaking into this world, and for the fullness of that kingdom to come quickly. Also pray for missionaries who are telling the life-changing gospel of Jesus and working for justice in the world.

5

WORDS

BIG IDEA

Our instinct is to speak and act impressively in service to God, but it is more important that we humbly listen to God.

BIBLE CONVERSATION *20 MINUTES*

Ecclesiastes 5 begins with wisdom about the words we say to God and how we handle the words he says to us. It describes a person going to the temple in Jerusalem to offer a vow. At first, this example may seem foreign to us, but as we shall see, our lives are full of similar situations. Have someone read **Ecclesiastes 5:1–7** aloud. Then discuss the questions below.

What do you notice about the attitude of a person who is rash to make ambitious vows, and how is it different from the attitude of one who listens instead?

How might these attitudes apply to attending worship or Bible studies today?

What do you think the foolish worshiper described here is trying to get for himself out of going to the temple? How does this compare to reasons why people today attend worship?

Imagine a non-believer saw the actions and attitudes of the foolish worshiper. Based on those actions, what might the non-believer think about God? What if the non-believer observed the wise worshiper?

****

Now read the article, "Get Real." Take turns by paragraph reading it aloud, and discuss the questions when you finish.

Lesson

ARTICLE

GET REAL

5 MINUTES

We are already known. Our evils are already found out. Our denials are less and less interesting. Clean and humble truth about God and about us is taking center stage. We are made quiet in the presence of a vibrant storyteller, an intimate lover, a merciful knower of our worst moments. The absence of haste rests us. Freed from having to spin words, contentment finds us. God is here. Finally, sanity and grace find us. We can rest now.

Zack Eswine, *Recovering Eden*

Chapter 5 of Ecclesiastes comes as both a welcome oasis and another sharp shock at this point in the book. It's a refreshing chapter because it makes clear—if we doubted it at all—that this Teacher is a devout believer in the God of Israel. There have been flashes of light in the earlier chapters, to be sure, but the atmosphere has been often bleak and even oppressive at times. But now we come to a chapter where God's presence in heaven is affirmed with clarity and the Teacher's sincere faith shines through: "but God is the one you must fear." In a broken world, the house of God, the temple, the new Eden on earth, stands as a beacon of hope and a beautiful refuge for the perplexed disciple in ancient Israel. God himself is there.

And yet, at the same time, it is not as simple as turning up and assuming all will be well simply because you made the effort to get out of bed that morning. There are clear warnings for each pilgrim: "Guard your steps when you go near to the house of God. . . . Be not rash with your mouth. . . . Let your words be few. . . . Let not your mouth lead you into sin." What is going on here?

As I write these words, our congregation in Aberdeen is on the verge of renovating one of the most wonderful church buildings in our city centre. In God's amazing kindness, we have the opportunity to plant a living Bible-preaching ministry in a new location, and we are enjoying strategizing about how to employ an overwhelming amount of space for gospel purposes. We don't believe that our building is God's temple. We know that the household of God is the people who, in our weekly Lord's Day services, gather with all the saints in the heavenly Jerusalem and we draw near to God together. But I have learned that in a building project it is unbelievably easy to envisage a church building for a world of activity and Christian hustle and bustle that can quickly distract and will eventually even destroy a living congregation of Christ's people.

We are geared to speak and to act much more than we are to listen. But *listening* to God—more than doing things for God—is the path of wisdom. Listening to God is the primary sacrificial act of spiritual worship of the true believer and it does not come naturally. We want to go it alone and do what we think needs to be done. The fall into sin in the garden of Eden, before it was ever a taking and a touching of forbidden fruit, was a failure to listen to the word of God.

For our own congregation, this has meant a liberating clarity to our building renovation plans: we are determined in every way to protect the pulpit as the primary location in the building. For it is in coming near to listen to God through the reading and preaching of his Word, above all the other voices of the world around us, and even (maybe especially) above ourselves and our own individual ideas, that we find the highway to life.

I find this a truly humbling intervention at this point in Ecclesiastes. If you're like me, you may be finding the Teacher's way of looking at life a little disorientating, and you may have plenty of questions. A major part of his message is that God's words carry more weight and significance and light than our words, which often betray our creaturely limitations and ignorance and proud presumptions. Why is it that we think we know best about how the world should work? Why do we so quickly think that just because something doesn't make sense to us, it therefore doesn't make sense? Why are we so often better at speaking than listening? Why are we keen to try and fix things instead of simply speaking to God in dependent prayer?

Ecclesiastes 5 adds more texture to the Teacher's portrait of life in God's world. He sees and knows everything, even the most secret parts of us. "God is in heaven and you are on earth" (v. 2). This simple phrase packs a punch. It instructs us that we are limited, time-bound, and frail while God is strong, eternal, and infinitely wise. So in the presence of absolute greatness, wise believers know to get real. They know to subordinate everything about themselves to all that God is and to learn, afresh, to trust and obey all that he says.

Take care every single time you go to church. Don't let habit and custom and familiar routine become rote and superficial. You are worshiping a holy God. As the Bible is read and expounded, know that "the word of God is living and active, sharper than any two-edged sword, piercing to the division of soul and of spirit, of joints and of marrow, and discerning the thoughts and intentions of the heart" (Hebrews 4:12). Be sure to listen more than you speak. Listen to God, and bend your knee in reverence to him.

DISCUSSION *10 MINUTES*

Describe some situations in which you tend to be more ready to do something for God than to listen to God.

Imagine you were less rash and listened better, especially in spiritual conversations or at church. What might be the benefit to you? To others?

DREAMERS, SPEAKERS, AND LISTENERS

20 MINUTES

Ecclesiastes 5:7 presents three ways to live. The first two are versions of self-effort and end in vanity: "When dreams increase and words grow many, there is vanity." The third is lasting: "But God is the one you must fear." Let's describe these three ways of living in terms of the habits that accompany them:

Habits of a here-and-now dreamer. "Dreams increase." Your habits reflect plans and dreams for pleasures and achievements in this world, or how you are hounded by the prospect of losing those things.

Habits of a hasty speaker. "Words grow many." Your habits reflect a desire to appear outwardly religious to yourself, God, and others, or to press ahead spiritually by your strong commitments.

Habits of a humble listener. "God is the one you must fear." Your habits reflect a posture of relying on God rather than impressing him, recognizing your creaturely dependence and his fatherly goodness.

On your own, read through each set of descriptions below. Most have to do with our habits when it comes to God's word (which we especially hear through the Bible, in preaching, and in certain other elements of worship). For each set, note the description that's <u>most true of you</u>. When the group is ready, discuss the questions at the end of the exercise.

❐ **Here-and-Now Dreamer.** My life is a constant striving to get ahead.

❐ **Hasty Speaker.** My life is a constant striving to prove myself to God or other believers.

❐ **Humble Listener.** My life is filled with rest and receiving from God, as Jesus proves himself faithful to me.

❐ **Here-and-Now Dreamer.** I find it hard to fit God's word (the Bible, preaching, worship) into my life.

❐ **Hasty Speaker.** I build time learning God's word into my life so I can be a high-performing Christian.

❐ **Humble Listener.** I build time under God's word into the rhythms of my life so it will renew me.

❐ **Here-and-Now Dreamer.** God's word is an interruption. It takes me away from my life—or worse, challenges it.

❐ **Hasty Speaker.** God's word is a burden. I usually don't enjoy being reminded of what more I need to do.

❐ **Humble Listener.** God's word is a gift. The Holy Spirit has lovingly prepared it for me.

❏ **Here-and-Now Dreamer.** I judge sermons by how practical they are.

❏ **Hasty Speaker.** I judge sermons by how theologically astute they are.

❏ **Humble Listener.** I allow sermons to judge me.

❏ **Here-and-Now Dreamer.** I don't necessarily expect much from Bible reading or a sermon.

❏ **Hasty Speaker.** I expect a good Bible study or sermon to help me learn how to speak more impressively about God.

❏ **Humble Listener.** I come to the Bible or a sermon expecting God to speak. My Father has much to say to me, his child.

❏ **Here-and-Now Dreamer.** I think my church is boring compared to other activities.

❏ **Hasty Speaker.** I think my church is better than other churches.

❏ **Humble Listener.** I think my church is beautiful because it's Jesus's church.

❏ **Here-and-Now Dreamer.** I am not satisfied with my ministry, mission, or church work unless I see results.

❏ **Hasty Speaker.** I feel insecure about my ministry, mission, or church work when results aren't evident.

❏ **Humble Listener.** My Father is teaching me much through both the ups and the downs of my ministry, mission, or church work.

❐ **Here-and-Now Dreamer.** Although I know he says otherwise, God feels uninvolved and distant when it comes to real life.

❐ **Hasty Speaker.** If I want God to come near and get involved, I need to make myself more worthy first.

❐ **Humble Listener.** I'm so glad God's word is true even when God feels distant.

Share some of your responses with the group. What patterns do you see in your life? What progress has God already worked in you? How is he lovingly speaking to you, right now, inviting you to enjoy the gift of his word in new ways?

WRAP-UP AND PRAYER *10 MINUTES*

Along with praying for other elements of your worship, a good exercise is to pray for your praying. Pray that your words to God would be humble, and that God's words to you would be "sweeter also than honey and drippings of the honeycomb" (Psalm 19:10).

NOTE: The next lesson skips ahead to Ecclesiastes 7. If you want to read through all of Ecclesiastes as a part of this study, read Ecclesiastes 5:8–6:12 on your own before the next time your group meets.

6

DEATH

BIG IDEA

Reflecting on death can help us loosen our grip on the empty promises of this world and open our hands to receive God's gifts.

BIBLE CONVERSATION *20 MINUTES*

Ecclesiastes 7 appears to be a collection of proverbs. But in the Teacher's clever style, many of the sayings are anti-proverbs. Rather than the expected congratulations upon the birth of a child or condolences upon the death of a loved one, he flips the script. Rather than selling us nostalgia about the old days or promises that wise choices will pay off in the long run, he invites us to question whether accepted wisdom is truly wisest.

Be aware that the advice in verse 15 to "be not overly righteous" probably does not refer to godly morality. More likely, the Teacher has in mind social, workplace, or judicial rules and expectations. Being careful to handle these matters correctly will not always mean you are rewarded for having done things the right way. In fact, being too meticulous about "right behavior" might have some destructive effects.

Have someone read **Ecclesiastes 7:1–25** aloud, or have several readers take turns. Then discuss the questions below.

When has entering a sad place been more satisfying to your heart than the laughter of a happy place? Why can a sad place be more satisfying?

Which anti-proverb in this passage might be a gift to you, helping you let go of a common but unhelpful way of thinking? Explain.

It's no surprise that being overly wicked might bring a life to ruin (v. 17), but consider the person who carefully follows right-behavior expectations. What might be going on in that "righteous" person's heart, and how might you "destroy yourself" that way?

✶✶✶✶

Now take turns reading this lesson's article aloud, switching readers at the paragraph breaks. When you finish, discuss the questions that follow.

ARTICLE

DEATH AND ITS GIFTS

5 MINUTES

There are worse things in the world than dying. For Ecclesiastes, it is a terrible tragedy to live without realizing that I am going to die. This is a strange way of thinking about death, but God has given it to us in this part of his Word for our good. Here are three strange faces of death in Ecclesiastes, each of which comes to us bearing life-giving gifts:

DEATH IS A SURGEON

In the opening poem of chapter 1, the word *death* is not used. But in lyrical tilt, with tidal ebb and flow, the rhythmical poetry is an ode to death's all-pervasive presence: "A generation goes, and a generation comes, but the earth remains forever" (1:4). The point of this poem is that the world itself seems to chase its tail and not get anywhere. Everything is cyclical, not linear. The Teacher uses creation to nail the paradox of life in this world: it is a place of permanent repetition *and* constant change. In a world of permanent repetition, where we end up doing the same old things, seven days a week, again and again, we long for something to interrupt it—a new job, a new relationship, a new house, a whole new chapter—then we die. And in a world of constant change, we long for something to give us permanence—the gym, the health plan, the insurance policy, the facelift—then we die.

Surgeons operate on human bodies. They wound and cut in order to heal and make whole. In Ecclesiastes, death is a cardiologist, the most skillful of heart surgeons. The great motivating desire of every human being is the desire for gain, for a surplus, for something left over that will last forever because of my life. We want to achieve something and be someone. And the greatest obstacle to our ambition is death. In his grace and mercy, God uses death to operate on our heart's anxieties and fears and on our restless striving and straining and toiling for gain, for greatness, and for a forever-after legacy which God has placed off-limits to fallen, rebellious creatures.

DEATH IS A PREACHER

One of the most striking verses in the whole of Ecclesiastes is 7:1, "A good name is better than precious ointment, and the day of death than the day of birth." Like the sound of nails screeching down a blackboard, our whole being recoils from the notion that the day a person dies is better than the day a baby is born. But the Teacher's point is that funerals and crematoriums and hearses and open graves and tears on the pillow at night are the amplifiers God uses to address a world obsessed with the trivial and the fleeting. "It is better to go to the house of mourning than to go to the house of feasting, for this is the end of all mankind, and the living will lay it to heart" (v. 2).

All preachers grapple with how to lay things to the heart: how to get us to feel, and see, and believe, and trust, and hope, and savor—not just with our head, but with every fiber of our being. Ecclesiastes knows that coffins lay things to the heart better than cribs. They're better preachers.

A new baby has life ahead of him or her, but what can we say about that baby yet? Not much. But sit a while in the next funeral you attend, and look and listen. What is said—and left unsaid—about the deceased person? Was she wise, generous, humble, transformed by grace? Did she love the Lord Jesus? Or did she spurn her Creator and live out her days as a satisfied squatter in a corner of the King's grounds, attending to her own puny empire?

What will be said about *you* when it's your turn to lie in the coffin as friends and family gather? Receive the gift of death's sermon. Lay it to heart. Today.

DEATH IS AN ARTIST

In Ecclesiastes 9, immediately after another reminder that everything done under the sun will come to an end for each of us, we are given a command: "Go, eat your bread with joy, and drink your wine with a merry heart, for God has already approved what you do." Death does not just destroy. It urges us to sketch life and light on the canvass of our lives while we can: "Let your garments always be white. . . . Enjoy life with the wife whom you love" (vv. 8–9).

The logic here is that death loosens my grip on God's gifts, as if they were ever mine by right, and instead frees me to see his world for what it is: the lavish endowment to wayward creatures of abundant good things we do not deserve. Death frees me to enjoy things for what they are rather than what I want them to be. Creation is there to be enjoyed and lingered over, not plundered for my gain or manipulated for my fame.

Food and drink, love and sex, work and beauty—these things become even more enjoyable when we paint them into our lives knowing one day they will pass. Try and hold on to them, or worship them, and we will find we are chasing the wind with only fistfuls of mist to show for all our effort.

In one hundred years it is almost certain no one will remember you ever lived. Think about that. If it's true, then here is Ecclesiastes' portrait of a life well lived: Open a nice bottle, and open your home. Share what you own. Give away what you have. Remember your Creator. Enjoy your loved ones. Fear God. Love his law. Treasure his gospel.

For it is treasuring what God has given you in Jesus that will reverse the priorities of the world around us (me first, take what you can get, keep what you can, strive for what you want) and make you radically different in your living (others first, give what you can, give away what you know you can't keep, be content with what you have). The gospel calls you to a life of knowing your heavenly Father in close personal relationship so that your every need—your *every* need!—is met by his good hand of providential care, not your two hands of restless toil.

Each of these things are God's great gifts. And, strangely, death can open your hands to receive them.

DISCUSSION *10 MINUTES*

In what ways have you felt death being a surgeon, preacher, or artist to you? Explain.

What is something in your life that's become more enjoyable because you've stopped trying to hold on to it? Or what is something that might become more enjoyable if you loosened your grip?

Lesson

EXERCISE

LOOSEN YOUR GRIP, OPEN YOUR HANDS

20 MINUTES

The article mentioned two practices the approach of death can work in you:

You can <u>loosen your grip</u> on the joys and honors of this world.

You can <u>open your hands</u> to receive the gifts of God.

These two habits work together: Loosening your grip helps you open your hands to enjoy God's gifts. And the joy of God's gifts helps you loosen your grip on lesser things.

For this exercise, you'll consider both where you need to loosen your grip and how you might open your hands. Work through both parts of the exercise on your own. When you're done, you'll have a chance to share with the group.

LOOSENING YOUR GRIP

Read through some needs you may feel that are described below. Note some places where you most tend to demand that this world give you satisfaction.

Enjoyment. "Life is sad, and I need some happiness." I'm desperate to keep happy moments coming, and I look for these . . .

❏ in my work, career, or education.

❏ through friends, relationships, or community.

❏ through my family, spouse, or children.

❏ in my ministry, Christian mission, or church commitment.

❏ in diversions, distractions, entertainment, or activities.

❏ other _____.

Appreciation. "I deserve some respect!" I want to be liked and valued, and I try to get it . . .

❏ through my work, career, or education.

❏ from friends, relationships, or community.

❏ from my family, spouse, or children.

❏ through my ministry, Christian mission, or church commitment.

❏ through diversions, distractions, entertainment, or activities.

❏ other _____.

Impact. "Things need to go my way." I'm hungry for control, and I want to leave a legacy or change things for the better . . .

❏ at work, school, or in my career.

❏ with my friends, relationships, or community.

❏ in my family, spouse, or children.

❑ in my ministry, Christian mission, or church commitment.

❑ in my diversions, distractions, entertainment, or activities.

❑ other _____.

Enjoyment. "Whoever dies with the most, wins." I'm trying to amass money or comforts, or hoping to build a future for myself...

❑ through my work, career, or education.

❑ by the right friends, relationships, or community.

❑ through my family, spouse, or children.

❑ through my ministry, Christian mission, or church commitment.

❑ in my diversions, distractions, entertainment, or activities.

❑ other _____.

Fulfillment. "If this is right, or if I do it right, it's supposed to satisfy me!" I am trying to feel good about myself, or somehow fulfilled in life . . .

❑ through my work, career, or education.

❑ in my friendships, relationships, or community.

❑ in my family, spouse, or children.

❑ by my ministry, Christian mission, or church commitment.

❑ through diversions, distractions, entertainment, or activities.

❑ other _____.

OPENING YOUR HANDS

Now, think about what you want to receive from God. Ecclesiastes will end by assuring us that its wisdom comes from our loving Shepherd (12:11). He opens our hands to receive his good gifts. Which gifts might especially help you loosen your grip on this world's empty promises? Complete some or all of the sentences below.

Gift of CONTENTMENT. Contentment from God allows you to enjoy what your Father gives in this life instead of resenting how he does not fill all your longings yet. "Now there is great gain in godliness with contentment, for we brought nothing into the world, and we cannot take anything out of the world" (1 Timothy 6:6–7).

I desire for my Father to make me content and joyful in how, already in this world, he has given me_____

_____

_____.

Gift of COMFORT. Spiritual blessings in Christ are sure gifts you already have if you believe in Jesus. One kindness of your Father is to comfort and encourage you by reminding you of these—gifts like his forgiveness, his approval of your right reputation in Jesus, your status as his child, the Holy Spirit's constant presence, your heart's new ability to love others, and more. "Restore to me the joy of your salvation" (Psalm 51:12).

I desire for my Father to loosen my grip on this world by giving me joy over how he has saved me, especially how he_____

_____

_____.

Gift of HOPE. Another gift is to see beyond this world to the fully realized joy, justice, satisfaction, and life with God that is yet to come. "I shall behold your face in righteousness; when I awake, I shall be satisfied with your likeness" (Psalm 17:15).

I desire for my Father to increase my hope in the next life, when he will give me_____

_____

_____.

When the group is ready, share some of your results and explain why you chose them. Where do you need to loosen your grip, and how do you want to open your hands?

WRAP-UP AND PRAYER *10 MINUTES*

One of the best ways to open your hands to receive God's gifts is to open your mouth in prayer. Pray together for the desires you identified in the exercise, and confess to your Father the places where you need to loosen your grip.

NOTE: If you want to read all of Ecclesiastes in order, read 7:26–8:17 on your own before your next group meeting. The next lesson will pick up with chapter 9.

7

LIFE

BIG IDEA

As we let go of self-importance and stop straining for self-achievement, we learn to truly live and enjoy God's gifts.

BIBLE CONVERSATION *20 MINUTES*

Ecclesiastes 9 opens with more frustrations: evil in the world, the sadness of death, and the fact that both good people and evil people seem to suffer equally from troubles God brings their way. But this chapter also endorses a response that is surprisingly celebratory about life. Have someone read **Ecclesiastes 9** aloud, or have several readers take turns, and then discuss the questions below.

Verses 1–6 begin by saying the righteous are "in the hand of God" as they suffer death and other troubles. Why might it be important to understand that these troubles reflect God's plan, not his neglect?

Verses 7–10 describe a person whose attitude about possessions, family life, and work is full of joy rather than marked by complaints and frustration. What might this person already understand about life, making such an attitude possible?

How might the example in verses 13–16 encourage you to follow the rest of this chapter's teaching?

****

Now take turns, by paragraph, reading the article aloud to the group. Then discuss the questions at the end of the article.

7

HOW TO LIVE

5 MINUTES

You say grace before meals. All right. But I say grace before the concert and the opera, and grace before the play and pantomime, and grace before I open a book, and grace before sketching, painting, swimming, fencing, boxing, walking, playing, dancing and grace before I dip the pen in the ink.

G. K. Chesterton

The strange and startling message of Ecclesiastes is that mortality does not mean morbidity. Looking long and hard at death can pave the road to life. Ecclesiastes 9 manages to encapsulate the message of the whole book by getting us to look, again, at death. But then it also gives us a wonderfully clear statement of how this helps us live.

When you plan your life, don't forget who you are and how little you control. Shepherds in the ancient world used goads, sticks with a sharp tip, to prod their animals in the right direction. The Teacher in Ecclesiastes wants his words to wound a little: "The words of the wise are like goads, and like nails firmly fixed are the collected sayings; they are given by one Shepherd" (12:11). He's saying that if he can get our hearts and minds to throb, it will make us sit up and take notice. So he gives us words to stop us in our tracks, turn us around, and get us going in the right direction.

We know we will die, but we live as if we will not. Ecclesiastes urgently wants us to stop living like this. The Teacher wants us to learn that all our disappointments in life are reminders of death, all our sorrows are echoes of the one great specter which fills the earth with futility: "It is the same for all, since the same event happens to the righteous and the wicked, to the good and the evil, to the clean and the unclean, to him who offers sacrifices and him who does not sacrifice." Death is the great equalizer. It stalks and claims its prey without discretion. For the Teacher, this brute fact is meant to help us remember what we are: morning mist, wisps of smoke, mere whispers on the wind. "As for man, his days are like grass; he flourishes like a flower of the field; for the wind passes over it, and it is gone" (Psalm 103:15–16).

This means we need to learn that we do not control the duration, the direction, or the achievements of our life. Things don't always follow a predictable course: "Again I saw that under the sun the race is not to the swift, nor the battle to the strong, nor bread to the wise, nor riches to the intelligent, nor favor to those with knowledge, but time and chance happen to them all. For man does not know his time" (vv. 11–12).

As I write these words, the COVID-19 pandemic continues to surge around the world. If it has taught us anything, it is that we are not in control of our lives. An invisible virus has brought mighty nations to a complete standstill and placed global economies into decline. Who had this in their diaries for the year 2020? The Teacher sees that our misty lives and our inability to control the future can make a life-altering difference in the present.

As you live your life, don't forget who God is and what he loves. Death can be the very thing that stops us from expecting too much of things that turn out only to disappoint us. Death can make us stop and savor a moment that would otherwise have passed us by—a moment at a table spread with food, in the presence of our spouse, in the company of our family, in the blessedness of work which satisfies both mind and body and creates wealth for the good of others. All is vanity only when we think "all" is all there is. If all is there because God put it there for now, for today, for me to use for others and for him, then in fact things eternal are shaping how we hold things temporal.

Take in the language of verses 7–10 and ponder their riches. Here we are told that God loves our loving of the good gifts in his world. He commands us, "Go" and says to eat and drink and be merry. Here is a profound reorientation to the simple things of life: we see them as sufficient for our well-being precisely because, in fact, we have come to understand they are not enough. These verses are a return to the guileless beauty of the garden Eden where the first command in the Bible was to be fruitful and multiply, and the second command was to eat from the trees of earth for food. This is how life was meant to be.

But we have made these divine gifts not enough for us. We think we deserve more. One of my favorite quotes from a biblical scholar is Derek Kidner's depiction of the fall: "This was the nerve the serpent had touched in Eden, to make even Paradise appear an insult."[6] We live like this a lot of the time—as if God's good gifts are not sufficient for us. Instead of seeing each and every morsel of food as undeserved mercy and a token of divine goodness, we rush through meals to get on with the really important stuff: the projects of our lives that we think we are controlling. We begin to take our relationships for granted, and a precious spouse becomes part of the wallpaper of our lives, not the object of daily pursuit in tender nourishment and attentive care.

When the English theologian J. I. Packer died, someone said of him that he lived slowly enough to think deeply about God. It is no coincidence that every personal account of interactions with Packer that was published in the days following his death commented on his gentleness and humility. He was unhurried in life because he knew the goodness of God, and therefore he gave others the attention a human life deserves.

Every time my feet touch the floor when I get out of bed in the morning it is an undeserved mercy. Every project in my diary for the week ahead should be given to God and surrendered to his perfect purposes: "For you are a mist that appears for a little time and then vanishes. Instead you ought to say, 'If the Lord wills, we will live and do this or that'" (James 4:14–15). Every task I contemplate should be considered in light of whether it will benefit mainly me or mainly others. Sometimes we are so full of our own plans that we just don't have time for humble, godly, generous, present goodness toward others.

If all of life is a gift from God, it means that all of life is meant to be offered back to God in gratitude and worship. I believe this is why at various points in the Bible storyline we are told that God does not desire sacrifice and burnt offering.* Burnt offerings relate to human guilt, but we know from Leviticus that there were also to be thanksgiving offerings as part of our worship. These offerings point back to what Adam in the garden of Eden was meant to give to God in a world without sin: the offering back to him of a life of overflowing gratitude and devotion.

This is how the world should have been and this is why the words of the Lord Jesus in Hebrews 10 are so beautiful: "Sacrifices and offerings you have not desired, but a body you have prepared for me. . . . Then I said, 'Behold, I have come to do your will, O God'"

---

* 1 Samuel 15:22; Psalms 40:6; 51:16; Hebrews 10:5–7

(Hebrews 10:5–7). A life of grateful praise is not incidental to our vocation as human beings but is, in fact, our very reason for living. The Lord Jesus is the exemplary Man, the second Adam, as he offers himself to his Father as a sacrifice of praise. In him, we too know God as our generous and loving Father and ourselves as dependent children.

As we live like this, we will begin to discern the bountiful and lavish care of our heavenly Father in a thousand locations where we are normally blind. We will find anxiety and boasting and restless striving receding in our hearts, and instead contentment, gratitude, and cheerful labor growing in their place.

DISCUSSION *10 MINUTES*

How well do your actions reflect an understanding that God is your Creator and you are a creature? What difference does that awareness make?

How have you been so full of your own plans that you neglect humble and present goodness to others? Or where has God taught you to set aside your plans and your striving, giving you room to be generous to others?

Lesson

EXERCISE

7

THE FULL-LIFE LIST
20 MINUTES

One lesson of Ecclesiastes is that to have a full life in this world, you must realize you can't create that full life for yourself. Furthermore, even the joys God gives you in this world will be mixed with frustrations, and are merely a taste of the greater full life to come. You need to learn this and rest in it. Then you will be free to see, enjoy, and thank your Father for the many gifts he gives you already today.

For this exercise, work on your own to make a list of gifts God provides for you today. Do this in three steps, described below. Then discuss your list when the group is ready.

Step 1: Read. Article 6 (in our previous lesson) ended with a diverse list of gifts God provides to us today. Read through that list below. Note some that are meaningful to you, or some that reveal where you tend to be blind to the care of your loving Father.

- The beauty of creation, worth lingering over
- Cheerful food and drink
- Love and sex
- Sharing and hospitality

- The desire to give away what you own
- Knowledge of your Creator
- Family and friends
- Reverence for God and a desire to obey him (yes, this is a *gift* from God)
- The comforts of the gospel

Step 2: Observe. Ecclesiastes 9:7–10 alludes to many of God's present-day gifts. Read that passage again below. From it, add to the list. You can add both gifts mentioned in the passage and gifts not directly mentioned but brought to mind by the passage. (It is not necessary to fill in every line.)

> Go, eat your bread with joy, and drink your wine with a merry heart, for God has already approved what you do.
>
> Let your garments be always white. Let not oil be lacking on your head.

Enjoy life with the wife whom you love, all the days of your vain life that he has given you under the sun, because that is your portion in life and in your toil at which you toil under the sun. Whatever your hand finds to do, do it with your might, for there is no work or thought or knowledge or wisdom in Sheol, to which you are going.

Step 3: Reflect. What other gifts that God has put in your life come to mind? These might be anything from the simplest pleasures to your most treasured joys or truths of the gospel. Add some to your list.

Now tell about some items from your list. Why did you put them on the list? Are you striving to hold on to them, or are you able to thank God for them and enjoy them as gift while they last?

WRAP-UP AND PRAYER *10 MINUTES*

Include thanksgiving for life's gifts in your prayer time together.

NOTE: If you are reading through all of Ecclesiastes, read chapter 10 on your own before your next group meeting, which will be a study of chapter 11.

8

PLANTING

BIG IDEA

As participants in God's kingdom, we approach our relationships in this world with the future in mind—planting seeds of care, compassion, and interest in others wherever we go.

BIBLE CONVERSATION *15 MINUTES*

Ecclesiastes 11 begins with the saying, "Cast your bread upon the waters." Whatever meaning this expression had in the ancient world has now been lost, but from the verses that follow we can gather that it likely has something to do making investments that will eventually bring a return. Gain begins with letting go of what you already have and casting it off. With this in mind, have someone read **Ecclesiastes 11:1–8** aloud. Then discuss the questions below.

Our most important investments are not financial or agricultural, but personal. What parts of this passage are good advice for when we invest in people by caring for them? Explain.

According to the passage, what are some things we don't know? How might this shape our attitude and approach to investing in others?

****

Read more about "sowing" into the lives of others in this lesson's article. Take turns reading the article aloud, switching readers for each paragraph. Then discuss the questions that follow.

ARTICLE

SOW BOUNTIFULLY

5 MINUTES

> Whoever sows sparingly will also reap sparingly, and who-
> ever sows bountifully will also reap bountifully.
>
> 2 Corinthians 9:6

The Christian life is about taking the long-term view. Tomorrow, not today, is the day of glory. Today is the cross, tomorrow the crown.

Ecclesiastes shares this perspective in its own distinctive way. The normal path, the worldly way—the foolish path—is to live for today only, whether due to fear or hopeless resignation about the future. The future is far off and unknown, but the present is immediate and real. To be sure, Ecclesiastes is not against living life to the full in the present, and this chapter is full of vibrant commands: cast, give, sow, rejoice, walk, remove vexation. But the main context for this hopeful action is that tomorrow's fruitfulness can, in God's good hands, flow from the fertility of today. This part of Ecclesiastes encourages us to make deliberate decisions and take concrete steps to send blessings into the future by what we do today.

We experience this in all the rhythms and seasons of life, maybe often without realizing it. I watch this happen every year as we celebrate Christmas. This season is all about the fruitfulness of gifts. Our love for those closest to us takes concrete form in the Advent season as we lavish that love on each other in the presents we give. But there is a connection between the sowing we have done earlier, in January through November, and the fruit of December. Many of the expressions of love and care we give or receive at Christmas are based on interactions we have had throughout the year.

If we have cherished a relationship all year round, it becomes especially precious in December. But if a relationship has been awkward and strained all year, in December it somehow becomes just a little more difficult or the distance becomes more noticeable and poignant. We sow all year, and at Christmas we reap the fruit of what we have sown. Seeds of care, nurture, and interest in others will sprout into joy and openness. Relationships gone awry will grow anger or resentment. Of course, not all bleakness is due to circumstances we control, but generally we reap what we sow.

Now take this principle and consider the whole course of our lives. If we look back on the kind of things we harvested in the last few years, or decade, we know how true it is that "whatever one sows, that will he also reap. For the one who sows to his own flesh will from the flesh reap corruption, but the one who sows to the Spirit will from the Spirit reap eternal life" (Galatians 6:7–8).

All who follow the Lord Jesus are gardeners. It is an unavoidable fact of spiritual life that we are always sowing, and in Galatians 5 the apostle Paul asks us to reflect on what kind of seeds we are planting. Sexual immorality, hatred, discord, jealousy, envy— these works of the flesh can be sown as tiny kernels but nourished into poisonous fruit that maims. Love, joy, peace, patience, kindness, goodness, faithfulness, gentleness and self-control—this fruit of the Spirit doesn't sprout out of thin air but flourishes from sowing to the Spirit. This happens in the considered decisions of our minds, the invisible affections of our hearts, and the visible daily actions of our lives.

Produce like this ripens when we sow death to ourselves and to our own selfish desires. A basic principle of horticulture is that death in the land leads to fruit in the hand. The road to resurrection and life always passes through crucifixion and death.

Gardeners take the long view. They know that today's painful toil will result in tomorrow's pleasant bounty. They know that small margins come to yield big differences, that little daily steps contribute to a long obedience in the same direction. They know that acts of love can beget a loveliness that is deep and endures for a lifetime.

The Teacher of Ecclesiastes knows this too with every fiber of his being. He knows there is a way of living that recognizes God has given us life as a sweet gift full of pleasant things to enjoy. He knows that while we're young and able we should live life to the full. But what should make our days full is sowing for tomorrow, and sowing morning and evening—in other words, sowing as much as we possibly can.

I want to encourage you, however this year finds you right now, to deliberately tend the orchards of your heart, your home and family, and your church family. Be a constant gardener. Intentionally find new behaviors to cultivate in each allotment, and begin to sow and nurture them.

Invest in God. Treasure his channels of grace in your gathered worship week by week: prayer and preaching of the Word, receiving the Lord's Supper. Sow to the flesh, and we will reap the whirlwind. Sow to the Spirit, and we will feast together. All year long, in each and every year that God gives, "let us not grow weary of doing good, for in due season we will reap, if we do not give up" (Galatians 6:9).

DISCUSSION *10 MINUTES*

How constant are you in your gardening—caring and showing interest in others? How might more constant care for others return pleasures to you?

How well do you look to the future, either the future in this life or in the next? What difference does it make in how you live now?

Lesson

EXERCISE

REACHING OUT TO OTHERS

25 MINUTES

To sow bountifully, you must be intentional. You will have to consider (1) where to sow, (2) what obstacles threaten to stop you, and (3) what encouragements of the gospel will spur you on. For this exercise, work through those three steps on your own first, and then share some of your results with the group when everyone is ready.

Step 1: Where might you sow, and to whom, and how? As you complete the rest of the exercise, it will help to have a specific place and people in mind, plus a specific way to care for them. Don't worry, no one is asking you to commit, just to imagine for a moment. Where could you see yourself investing in others?

- The *where* might be as nearby as your own home, neighborhood, workplace, or church, or it could be as far away as a foreign mission field.

- The *who* could range from specific people you know well to people you've never met from an unfamiliar culture.

- The *how* could mean preaching or telling about Jesus, serving his kingdom as it overcomes troubles in the present world, or investing in people through some other kindness—even something that seems small on the surface.

I imagine myself sowing in (*where*)_____,

to (*who*)_____,

by (*how*)_____.

Step 2: What obstacles within you threaten to stop you? The article mentioned some common reasons why you might instead live for yourself and for today. To better understand your inner obstacles, rank them (1, 2, 3, etc.) in order of how likely you think they would be to keep you from your sowing mission.

_____ **Fear.** I am wary of Jesus's call for me to take up my cross and die. I don't just mean martyrdom; I fear death to my comforts, my pride, my record of achievements, my reputation for success, and my self-reliance.

_____ **Resignation.** I don't think I have it in me, nor do I think much can change through me. There are too many barriers—in me, in others, or in the world. My sowing idea just doesn't feel worthwhile or wise to implement right now.

_____ **Coldness.** The things of God, and Jesus's kingdom, feel far off compared to my own needs today. I don't feel the love for God and others that I'm supposed to feel to invest in others with joy. I'd probably just end up resentful.

_____ **Attachment.** Going often means leaving other things and other people, perhaps things and people I love. I don't think I could do that.

_____ **Other:** _____

Step 3: How might the gospel encourage you? The good news of grace, telling you how fully Jesus saves you, will compel you to show that grace to others. Your salvation includes many powerful blessings, all equally sure. But to help yourself think through them, rank some of these blessings by how encouraging they feel to you today, or by your desire to appreciate them more.

_____ **Adoption.** I enjoy the supreme honor, daily companionship, and constant care of being a child of my heavenly Father. He lovingly sees to all my needs and powerfully works even beyond this time-bound world. "Therefore do not be anxious, saying, 'What shall we eat?' or 'What shall we drink?' or 'What shall we wear?'" (Matthew 6:31).

_____ **Righteousness.** In Christ, I have the best possible approval: God's acceptance through the righteous record I've received from Jesus, who died for my sin. I can live in gratitude instead of under pressure to be good enough. "Who is to condemn? Christ Jesus is the one who died—more than that, who was raised—who is at the right hand of God, who indeed is interceding for us" (Romans 8:34).

_____ **Holiness.** By the Holy Spirit's work in me, I am already dead to selfish striving. I can be confident: I *do* have a heart that's able to care for others. "Present yourselves to God as those who have been brought from death to life, and your members to God as instruments for righteousness. For sin will have no dominion over you" (Romans 6:13–14).

_____ **God's kingdom.** My outreach is a piece of something lasting because it witnesses for Jesus and is part of ushering in his kingdom. "Be steadfast, immovable, always abounding in the work of the Lord, knowing that in the Lord your labor is not in vain" (1 Corinthians 15:58).

_____ **Eternal life.** Whatever I have in this life has always been fleeting anyway. My eyes are on the forever blessings at my Savior's side in glory. "This light momentary affliction is preparing for us an eternal weight of glory beyond all comparison, as we look not to the things that are seen but to the things that are unseen. For the things that are seen are transient, but the things that are unseen are eternal" (2 Corinthians 4:17–18).

Now discuss your responses. What obstacles are within you, and how does the gospel answer them?

WRAP-UP AND PRAYER *10 MINUTES*

The nearness of your Father, through prayer, is one of the blessings of the gospel. Make use of it by praying about your opportunities to care for others. Confess your inner obstacles, ask for a caring heart, give thanks for the gospel, beg for a big harvest.

9

AGING

BIG IDEA

We should take advantage of our youth, enjoying and serving our Creator, because old age is coming soon and presents difficulties—though it too is a time to draw near to God.

BIBLE CONVERSATION *20 MINUTES*

The Teacher has shown us that life in this world is but a mist, and that loosening our grip on it frees us to live and to love, and to give and look above. Now he closes his discourse with a return to the topic of death.

His words are directed to young people, but are about getting old. Much of the passage is a symbolic picture of aging, and many of the symbols seem clear: grinders that "cease because they are few" probably refers to lost teeth, and a blossoming almond tree probably means graying hair. Other metaphors are less clear, but it is not necessary to figure them out, only to see that age takes its toll. Have someone read **Ecclesiastes 11:9–12:8** aloud. Then discuss the questions below.

What feelings that come with aging are evoked by this passage's language? Have you had some of those feelings, or do you fear going through them someday? Explain.

What is the passage's message to young people? What parts of it might be hardest for young people to understand and accept?

People sometimes think they should put off missionary work or other service to Christ's kingdom until they are older. Based on this passage, how might the Teacher argue against that?

****

Now take turns reading the article aloud, switching readers at each paragraph break. When you finish, discuss the questions that follow.

ARTICLE

BEFORE YOU COME UNDONE

5 MINUTES

> [God is] a hedonist at heart. All those fasts and vigils and stakes and crosses are only a façade. . . . Out at sea, out in His sea, there is pleasure, and more pleasure. . . . He has a bourgeois mind. He has filled His world full of pleasures. There are things for humans to do all day long without Him minding in the least. [A senior devil, Wormwood, "complaining" to a junior devil about how God really approves of humans enjoying life.]
>
> C. S. Lewis, *The Screwtape Letters*

They say that youth is wasted on the young. But this never makes sense to the young.

I am in precarious midlife-crisis time. I run with my children and compete physically with my sons. I claim I am trying to teach them the benefits of exercise and sport, while secretly I am evaluating whether their sporting prowess now outstrips my own. I grieve for what I'm losing even as I delight in what they are gaining. And as I try to explain to them how they need to enjoy every moment of these days, I can watch my words going in one ear and out the other. William Hazlitt said that death and old age for the young are "words without meaning." Death is like a dream. "To be young is to be as one of the Immortals."[7] Old age and death happen to other people, not them.

So what does Ecclesiastes have to say about this? I hope it is clear by now that the main message of this bewildering book in the Bible is that life must not be wasted on the living. Those who have life in their bodies should receive it as an unmerited divine gift and take every moment as an opportunity to live lives that glorify God to the utmost. This includes enjoying every part of the world in every way possible.

In Ecclesiastes 12, the young are told, "Remember also your Creator in the days of your youth, before the evil days come and the years of draw near of which you will say, 'I have no pleasure in them.'" In admonishing our young, I think we have tended to focus on the idea of remembering the Creator without realizing as well that in chapter 12 the repeated word is *before*. The young are encouraged to live a certain way before old age strikes. In a sense, rather than being able to somehow grasp the reality of their own old age in advance, those with youth on their side simply need to grasp life with both hands while they can. They need to do it before it is too late.

In the world of Ecclesiastes, such living is its own reward. The Teacher is trying to prevent a nursing home full of faithful believers whose regretful mantra is *if only*. My task as a parent is to show my children how wide and good and full and beautiful God's world is, and to live and speak in such a way that I invite them to explore all its depths with a happy heart. In this way, old age will take care of itself.

At the same time, the reality of aging is expressed here in a powerful, poetic way. Like a once majestic house falling into disrepair, so human beings find that in entering old age there is a sense in which life goes back on itself. We know this with the exchange that takes place in patterns of care and dependence, as parents who once cared for helpless babies in turn become vulnerable and are now cared for by their adult children.

But Ecclesiastes expresses all of this with evocative poetry, and we need to catch the details. Notice how in verse 2 all the objects of created light grow dark "before the sun and the light and the moon and the stars are darkened." Iain Provan points out that this is unusual language, for these burning lights do not ever themselves grow dark in our earthly cycle. Rather something more dramatic is being pictured here: "This is the language of the unmaking of creation."[8]

In Ezekiel 32:7–8, God uses this language to describe his judgment on the Pharaoh of Egypt. The sense, then, here in Ecclesiastes is that death is always a reminder of the bitterness of the curse pronounced on humanity in the garden of Eden. Instead of the goodness of the world and the beauty of life and fruitfulness, death is now present and pervasive and it causes creation itself to shudder into reverse. Death unmakes what God has made. What God has done in life becomes undone in death.

In all of this, the Teacher wants us to know that God is present and real. He has not abandoned us. In death, "the dust returns to the earth as it was, and the spirit returns to God who gave it." So with this perspective, it is possible to embrace the life we have been given as fully as we can without having to fear the future when we will be feeble and frail.

The Bible certainly says this period of our lives is inevitable, if we live long enough, and it will be a time when we believe that it was better to be young! But it is not a time when God is absent. Those who belong to the Lord Jesus know that the keys of Death and Hades belong to him.* Keys are symbols of access and power. The person with the keys wins. Jesus has ransacked the grave of its terror and power by entering it himself and emerging victorious on the other side.

We can enter old age with our very weakness and increased dependence on God being a lived-out sermon to the world around us that creation is good and meant to be enjoyed. There are few things more beautiful than families and Christian communities where the young learn from the old what it means to be young wisely, and where the old rejoice in the exuberance and experiences of the youths in their midst.

DISCUSSION *10 MINUTES*

In your youth, what wisdom did you learn from older believers?

Do you think the weakness and loss experienced in old age are likely to draw you closer to God or push you away? Explain why, and tell what habits in your life might make a difference.

---

* Revelation 1:18

RESPONSES TO GROWING OLD

20 MINUTES

Ecclesiastes 12 gives a picture of aging that is honest about its unpleasantness while also aware of its blessings. In this exercise, you will think about five realities of aging—some unpleasant and some encouraging—and possible ways to respond to them. Work through the exercise on your own first, and then discuss the questions at the end as a group.

If you consider yourself OLD (that is, if you are feeling the effects of aging and have begun to realize how short your time is), note all the responses that fit how you have reacted to aging.

If you consider yourself YOUNG (you haven't felt many effects of aging and tend to think you still have a long life ahead of you), think of how you react to other sobering events in life and try to imagine where you are headed. How do you see yourself responding to aging when it happens? Note all responses that fit.

Fear. Aging brings worry and fear about the unknown, the end of this life, our decline in abilities, the pain and indignities of the process of dying, and more. How do/might you respond?

☐ I seldom worry about this aspect of aging.

☐ I often worry about this aspect of aging.

☐ This reminds me to enjoy and serve God while I can.

☐ This makes me feel bitter or withdrawn. I pull away from God or others.

☐ This draws me closer to others.

☐ This draws me closer to God. It makes me depend on him more.

☐ This draws me closer to God. I become more focused on eternal things.

☐ Other: _____.

Sense of loss. Aging brings sadness over what we have lost or seem about to lose: freedom, strength, health, mental acuity, the ability to contribute, family and friends who are gone, and more. How do/might you respond?

☐ I seldom feel this aspect of aging.

☐ I often feel this aspect of aging.

☐ This reminds me to enjoy and serve God while I can.

☐ This makes me feel bitter or withdrawn. I pull away from God or others.

☐ This draws me closer to others.

☐ This draws me closer to God. It makes me depend on him more.

☐ This draws me closer to God. I become more focused on eternal things.

❏ Other: _____.

Weakness. Aging weakens both our bodies and our minds, and we become dependent on others for things we used to do easily. How do/might you respond?

❏ I seldom think about this aspect of aging.

❏ I often think about this aspect of aging.

❏ This reminds me to enjoy and serve God while I can.

❏ This makes me feel bitter or withdrawn. I pull away from God or others.

❏ This draws me closer to others.

❏ This draws me closer to God. It makes me depend on him more.

❏ This draws me closer to God. I become more focused on eternal things.

❏ Other: _____.

Mature wisdom. Aging clarifies many things about life, giving us wisdom we didn't have when we were younger. It can be a time of life when we slow down, enjoy God's gifts, share freely, and care well for others. How do/might you respond?

❏ I seldom think about this aspect of aging.

❏ I often think about this aspect of aging.

❏ This reminds me to enjoy and serve God while I can.

❏ This causes me to pull away from God or others.

❏ This draws me closer to others.

❏ This draws me closer to God. It makes me depend on him more.

❏ This draws me closer to God. I become more thankful and worshipful.

❏ Other: _____.

Redemption excitement. Aging brings us to the cusp of death, a major event in the story of our redemption. Death makes it oh-so-clear that we are sinners under a curse, rescued only by the grace of the Savior who has the power to raise the dead and is about to yank us out of this world and into glory. How do/might you respond?

❏ I seldom think about this aspect of aging.

❏ I often think about this aspect of aging.

❏ This reminds me to enjoy and serve God while I can.

❏ This causes me to pull away from God or others.

❏ This draws me closer to others.

❏ This draws me closer to God. It makes me depend on him more.

❏ This draws me closer to God. I become more thankful and worshipful.

❏ Other: _____.

When the group is ready, share and explain some of your results. What patterns do you notice? What might you still need to learn from Ecclesiastes?

If your group includes both old and young people, you might compare the differences in responses between the two groups. What should the young learn from the old now, before it's too late?

WRAP-UP AND PRAYER *10 MINUTES*

Jesus knows the sadness that comes from approaching death. Hebrews 2:14–15 tells us, "Since therefore the children share in flesh and blood, he himself likewise partook of the same things, that through death he might destroy the one who has the power of death, that is, the devil, and deliver all those who through fear of death were subject to lifelong slavery." Pray that God would help you draw near to your Savior who alone frees you from both the power and the fear of death, and that you would grow old with joy, hope, and freedom.

ETERNITY

BIG IDEA

The message of Ecclesiastes draws our hearts to eternity and to the surprising joys of God's commands and his coming judgment.

BIBLE CONVERSATION *20 MINUTES*

The final section of Ecclesiastes is an encouragement to take the Preacher's words seriously. It mentions goads, which you may remember are sticks with sharp tips used to prod livestock in the right direction. Goads are uncomfortable, but necessary and ultimately helpful. With this in mind, have someone read **Ecclesiastes 12:9–14**. Then discuss the questions below.

According to this passage, why has it been important to learn the Preacher's teachings? What reasons might you add?

Which of the teachings in Ecclesiastes has been a goad to you? Explain.

Why would the book end with a reminder of the sureness of God's judgment? Think of several ways that could encourage you to heed the book's wisdom.

****

Read the article now, taking turns by paragraph to read it aloud. Then discuss the questions that follow the article.

Lesson

ARTICLE

LOSE NOT THE THINGS ETERNAL

5 MINUTES

> No longer will evil be called good and good evil; no longer will darkness be turned into light and light into darkness; no longer will bitter be made sweet and sweet bitter (Isaiah 5:20). The conflict between good and evil will come to an end, as will all arguments about motives, intentions, and the nature of good.... Error will be exposed; real error, turning away from the Lord.
>
> G. C. Berkouwer, *The Return of Christ*

In his famous sermon, "Learning in War-Time," C. S. Lewis wrestled profoundly with the relationship between things temporal and things eternal. The particular pressure point in his context was the advent of the Second World War. How should his students make sense of the pursuit of academic pleasures—what Lewis called "placid occupations"—while Europe was poised on the precipice of so great a conflict?

Lewis engaged the question by widening its lens, dramatically broadening the scope from the immediate danger to the more remote but greatest reality of all: judgment by the living God.

If learning in wartime may be compared to Nero fiddling while Rome burned, then "to a Christian the true tragedy of Nero must be not that he fiddled while the city was on fire but that he fiddled on the brink of hell."[9] In other words, Lewis suggested, the real question is: how should we make sense of anything at all in our present, bodily, earthly lives while the yawning chasm of eternity waits for us beyond the grave?

Widening the lens usually changes everything. It's not that the questions and challenges disappear; rather, they come into sharper focus. When we're asking about the meaning of life, about whether anything matters, about why we should love and be loved if one day we will die, and about how we can continue to put one step in front of another when grief and pain threaten to suffocate our very lives, then the need for a big picture that is both true and beautiful is very urgent indeed.

In these studies, I have been suggesting that the skillful Teacher in Ecclesiastes helps us pass through things temporal with wisdom and wit precisely because he has seen the weight of things eternal. Ecclesiastes is the book in the Bible that asks some of the biggest questions in life but perplexes us with its seemingly unorthodox and impenetrable answers. We recall the question with which the Teacher opens his book: "What does man gain by all the toil at which he toils under the sun?" His whole aim in writing an answer to that question has been to help us to pass through things temporal (under the sun) that we finally lose not the things eternal (God has put eternity into man's heart).

The Teacher has tried to change our perspective on these days under the sun. First, he wants us to know our place as created beings under the care of our wise Creator. We grieve, as all grieve, but not as those without hope. We groan, like the Lord Jesus himself groaned when he saw the effects of the fall and the sin of hypocrites (see Mark 7:34 and 8:12), but we groan in hope. For our perspective is this: "Fear God and keep his commandments, for this is the whole duty of man."

This doesn't come naturally to us. We have hopes and dreams and aims and ambitions, and in the midst of these we think of our responsibilities to others: to spouses, children, parents, work colleagues, friends. But the Teacher tells us that every single duty or responsibility I have toward anyone else I have toward God first and foremost. Far from being nihilistic, the Teacher rather is endorsing the same worldview espoused by Moses and the Lord Jesus himself: that what God requires is love and obedience toward him, and love for neighbor as ourselves. This is simply what it means to be a created being. We think it means having all the answers and knowing why we hurt and why we lose, but in fact I was made to fear God, not to be God.

Second, the Teacher wants our perspective on time to be anchored in eternity—especially how eternity invades the present with the hope of judgment. Judgment can be a promise or a predicament, a hope or a fear, all depending on how we approach it. Ecclesiastes is in harmony with the biblical theme of judgment as a reason for jubilation. It is the hope of a world restored, causing that world itself to break out beyond its physical restraints in exultant praise.

> Let the rivers clap their hands;
>   let the hills sing for joy together
> before the LORD, for he comes
>   to judge the earth.
> He will judge the world with righteousness,
>   and the peoples with equity. (Psalm 98:8–9)

Life in light of eternity makes life truly livable. This is because, as Ecclesiastes has shown us so pointedly, some things simply have no answer in this life. One of the hardest things about Ecclesiastes is learning to accept its thesis that silence is the only available response to certain traumas. Some terror exceeds the capacity of some to bear it. "Again I saw all the oppressions that are done under the sun. And behold, the tears of the oppressed, and they had no one to comfort them! . . . And I thought the dead who are already dead more fortunate than the living who are still alive. But better than both is he who has not yet been" (4:1–3). We moderns are so poor at staring long and hard at brokenness that when a believer does this, and tells us how he feels, other Christians say he must not be a believer! In reality, however, he is simply expressing the shattering awfulness of life east of Eden.

Yet doing all this, the Teacher is goading us to prepare for judgment and to long for it with every fiber of our being. We cannot put an end to evil nor explain why natural disasters arrive unannounced, or how terrorism blights our globe with cruelty that seems to belong to a bygone age despite our best efforts at peace and reconciliation. But all is not vanity. For judgment is coming and the world will be remade. "Behold, I am making all things new" (Revelation 21:5).

DISCUSSION *10 MINUTES*

Where in your life do you need to learn to fear God, not try to be God? Explain.

How good are you at "staring long and hard at brokenness," or at allowing others to do so? Explain.

10

EXERCISE

ETERNITY AND MISSION

20 MINUTES

The gospel includes the promise of a coming life in the new heavens and new earth. The Bible says it will be a life of joy in part because of judgment—because Jesus will have judged and excluded all evil. Like other parts of the gospel, this truth is vital to us as we go out to love others or engage in mission. The assurance of a coming world where evil has been judged both compels us outward in the first place and comforts us when life on mission feels burdensome.

On your own, read through the Bible passages below that speak of the world and judgment to come. Note some truths or phrases that encourage you, then use them to complete the sentences at the end of the exercise.

Passage #1: In this lesson's Bible passage, the Preacher summarizes his teaching about how to live with eternity in mind:

> Fear God and keep his commandments, for this is the whole duty of man. For God will bring every deed into judgment,

with every secret thing, whether good or evil. (Ecclesiastes 12:13–14)

Passage #2: As mentioned in the article, Psalm 98 is a celebration of the day when Jesus will return as Judge of the whole world:

> Let the sea roar, and all that fills it;
>> the world and those who dwell in it!
> Let the rivers clap their hands;
>> let the hills sing for joy together
> before the LORD, for he comes
>> to judge the earth.
> He will judge the world with righteousness,
>> and the peoples with equity. (Psalm 98:7–9)

Passage #3: The prophet Isaiah envisions the day when believers will feast with Jesus, recognizing both the joy of God's multinational people and his judgment on his enemies:

> He will swallow up on this mountain
>> the covering that is cast over all peoples,
>> the veil that is spread over all nations.
>> He will swallow up death forever;
> and the Lord GOD will wipe away tears from all faces,
>> and the reproach of his people he will take away from
>> all the earth,
>> for the LORD has spoken.
> It will be said on that day,
>> "Behold, this is our God; we have waited for him, that
>> he might save us.
>> This is the LORD; we have waited for him;
>> let us be glad and rejoice in his salvation."
> For the hand of the LORD will rest on this mountain,
>> and Moab shall be trampled down in his place,
>> as straw is trampled down in a dunghill. (Isaiah 25:7–10)

Passage #4: The end of the Bible describes the new Jerusalem where Jesus will live with his people while evil is kept out:

> "Behold, I am coming soon, bringing my recompense with me, to repay each one for what he has done. I am the Alpha and the Omega, the first and the last, the beginning and the end.
>
> Blessed are those who wash their robes, so that they may have the right to the tree of life and that they may enter the city by the gates. Outside are the dogs and sorcerers and the sexually immoral and murderers and idolaters, and everyone who loves and practices falsehood." (Revelation 22:12–15)

Application. Now, pick thoughts or phrases from those Bible passages to complete the following sentences.

When life brings me face-to-face with injustice or sadness, I can be encouraged by the truth that . . .

When my work for Jesus's church or his kingdom brings opposition or takes me into places where there is injustice, I can be encouraged by the truth that . . .

God's plan for eternity motivates me to go out and care for others when I read that . . .

God's plan for eternity compels me to be part of his mission, serving Jesus's church and his kingdom, when I read that . . .

When the group is ready, share some of your responses and explain why you chose them.

WRAP-UP AND PRAYER *10 MINUTES*

Pray that the lessons of Ecclesiastes would stick with you and that God would continue to use it to work faith and repentance in you. You might want to use the following section of Psalm 103 as a springboard to your Ecclesiastes-themed prayer:

> As for man, his days are like grass;
>   he flourishes like a flower of the field;
> for the wind passes over it, and it is gone,
>   and its place knows it no more.
> But the steadfast love of the LORD **is from everlasting to everlasting on those who fear him,**
>   and his righteousness to children's children,
> to those who keep his covenant
>   and remember to do his commandments.
> The LORD **has established his throne in the heavens,**
>   and his kingdom rules over all. (Psalm 103:15–19)

LEADER'S NOTES

These notes provide some thoughts and background information that relate to the study's discussion questions, especially the Bible conversation sections. The discussion leader should read these notes before the study begins. Sometimes, the leader may want to refer the group to a point found here.

However, it is important that you not treat these notes as a way to look up the "right answer." You are studying Ecclesiastes, which invites you to slowly ponder the wisdom it presents. The best answers usually will be those the group discovers on its own through reading and thinking about the Bible text. You will lose the value of taking time to look thoughtfully at the text if you are too quick to turn to these notes.

LESSON 1: WISDOM

In addition to wondering about Ecclesiastes's author, your group may have questions about the book's strange title. Some might note that *Ecclesiastes* sounds like words we use to denote church functions, such as *ecclesiastical*. But like many other Bible books, Ecclesiastes is named for its author. The Preacher (or Teacher) literally means "instructor of the assembly" or "assembler of a group of students." The English title *Ecclesiastes* comes from the Preacher's name in Greek, which is similar to the Greek root we use in words about the church, the assembly of God's people.

The Preacher bases his claim that all is vanity on a wide range of observations, from scientific study of the earth to the fact that the sights and sounds of the world are never enough to satisfy—we keep wanting more. Both Christians and unbelieving optimists might initially react by claiming there *is* lasting change and all is not in vain. Indeed, other parts of the Bible do affirm that in Christ there is newness and real impact. But do not allow this to divert you from the hard truth that, even for Christians, life in this world is filled with vanities and much of what we long for is like a mist. Being Christians should make us all the more willing to admit this, so allow Ecclesiastes to speak.

Among the deep longings this passage alludes to are the desires not to leave this world, to have lasting impact on the world, to see our work not come undone, to have experiences that fully satisfy, to enjoy things new and novel, and to be remembered here after we are gone. Many people approach death with these in mind. Realizing they are out of our grasp, and asking us to consider how this affects the way we live on our road to death, is a long process behind the whole book of Ecclesiastes.

LESSON 2: HAPPINESS

At first glance, it might seem as if the Teacher is inconsistent about wisdom, praising it in one sentence and denouncing it as vanity in the next. But in fact, he has thought deeply about one of life's most frustrating truths: we can acquire great wisdom and learn to being highly sensible—which is better than being a fool—but even then, we will die and our wisdom will vanish. The puzzles we start to figure out will puzzle the next generation again. Gains in one era are lost in the next. A person hailed as brilliant is forgotten once he is gone. And wisdom passed on to our children often gets ignored or goes unappreciated.

The self-indulgences and achievements tried by the Teacher remain familiar to us today: food and drink, creative endeavors, houses and gardens, impressive families and workplaces, having people work under us, riches, entertainment, and sex. The impulse to indulge whatever our eyes desire and whatever our hearts find pleasure in (2:10) is as common today as it was for the Teacher—and still ends in vanity.

Even skillful work that produces beauty will not last. In time, it must be handed over to a person who might be less skillful or will not appreciate the beauty. Most of us can relate to the sense of loss in having to hand off a job to someone who might ruin things or giving the fruit of our labor to someone who barely understands what went into it.

LESSON 3: TIME

Many items in the list of life's happenings and chores are not things we would normally say are beautiful. In fact, several of them stem from sin in the world and the resulting curse. Yet, this passage is full of awareness of the absolute sovereignty of God over all things: God gives us our work (v. 10), controls the seasons of life (v. 11), has eternal plans that are unsearchable (v. 11), sees his works endure changelessly (v. 14), is unaffected by time (v. 15), and will judge even hidden evils (v. 16). For his people, our God makes "all things work together for good" (Romans 8:28). Resting in this comfort, there is a sense in which believers can find beauty in every rhythm and season God brings into our lives.

Verses 14 and 15 also might feel different to believers than they do to unbelievers. Believers can take comfort in knowing that God's love for them today will endure forever, since he does not change. And in contrast to the temporary nature of the world we live in now, the works of God and life with him endure forever. But unbelievers might read this passage as some sort of fatalism, leading only to the despairing thought that nothing can ever change. Indeed, apart from God there is only despair.

It's common for us to look at injustices or at death and have doubts that such horrible things could ever be undone. From our time-bound perspective, we see only hurts that will not heal and decaying bodies. Rather than pretend such sobering observations do not exist, Ecclesiastes invites us to ponder them so deeply that we finally look beyond our world—beyond time itself—to the reversals only a timeless God can fashion.

LESSON 4: JUSTICE

When we consider life "under the sun" in this world, the bleak perspective of Ecclesiastes 4:1–3 is refreshingly honest. Rather than pretend that oppression is not so bad and people don't suffer much from the advantage-taking of others, the Preacher invites us to see that injustice is constant and victims seldom receive much comfort. Christians should be quick to affirm that this is true of our sin-soaked world, even in places that are relatively prosperous and have much we rightly admire.

Still, all is not gloomy where Christ's kingdom breaks into our world. Believers are a people on mission, and when we work for justice we are "testifying to the kingdom of God" (Acts 28:23) with deeds that are a taste of the full kingdom of perfect justice Jesus will bring when he returns. To use a popular phrase, the kingdom is "already, and not yet." We should recognize both the bleakness of continued injustice (an awareness Ecclesiastes specializes in) and the splashes of coming justice we already see.

Working together, overcoming envy, accepting advice, and other humble-heart attitudes are indeed an answer for oppression. But this is not an answer we have the power to manufacture; rather, heart change is a work of God. And like his kingdom, his sanctifying work in us is "already, and not yet." We are learning to act with justice now, but will only do so fully in the next life.

LESSON 5: WORDS

The fool's attitude to worship is ultimately self-serving and proud. He is concerned with his sacrifice—with how impressive it might look or feel, or with how it might spur him on to some religious commitment in life. Although commitment to God is good, the fool has forgotten his place. He has forgotten that he is a creature standing before his Creator. He has forgotten to "be silent, all flesh, before the LORD" (Zechariah 2:13). He does not listen because he is presumptuous rather than teachable.

The fool is so focused on her own contribution that she cannot even see how, because of her self-confidence, her worship becomes an act of evil (Ecclesiastes 5:1). It is no surprise that she ends up not fulfilling all that she rashly vowed. The ability to serve God amid the difficulties and temptations of the world does not come from willpower but from humbly receiving his power.

Our worship can easily become about how we look or how it makes us feel. Some of us attend for appearances, remaining cold inside. Others of us pander to emotionalism or the quality of our experience. And all of us are in danger of being self-congratulatory over how our worship or our church is purer and avoids such sins. In every case, we have forgotten that "God is in heaven and you are on earth" (v. 2).

Because worship services so easily become occasions for judgmentalism, irritation, hypocrisy, or "just going through the motions," it helps to prepare our hearts beforehand. Guarding our steps when we go into the house of the Lord might include praying about our attitude or expectantly asking God to speak to us during worship. A good rule is to be thankful for what God provides through a church's worship services rather than bitter over what he withholds. We are first of all there to hear God's voice (spoken through human representatives) rather than mere human voices, including our own.

As in the Preacher's time, we have many foolish worshipers today: brash, opinionated, unthankful, quickly forgetful of God once they leave church. When we are like this, it doesn't just hurt us. It also hinders our ability to be winsome people who credibly share our faith. If we wish for others to explore their own relationship with God, we must pay attention to how we worship.

EXERCISE: This lesson points out the difference between religious striving and faith. One message throughout Ecclesiastes is that striving and self-effort are not the means to achievement. This is true even when we wish to achieve greater godliness. The rest of the Bible agrees, and prescribes a different means to godliness: faith. The striving described in Ecclesiastes is incompatible with faith. Striving relies on self-effort, while faith relies on Jesus. Striving summons gumption, while faith prays for the Spirit. Striving performs for God, while faith receives from God. There is a place for effort in the Christian life, but Christian effort is always rooted in God's strength, not our self-assured striving.

LESSON 6: DEATH

Laughter and happy places are often distractions more than they are true joy. Entering into a sad situation can be more authentic. It can teach us to let go of the empty promises of this world. It might help us confront nagging fears we've been trying not to think about. It often lets us comfort and come near to others in ways that are not possible when everyone is "having fun." And it ought to prod us to come nearer to God, the source of true joy. So it is not surprising that we often find sad situations more satisfying than happy ones.

While right behavior generally turns out better than evildoing, many of our right-behavior practices are not necessarily a part of true godliness. We may practice right behavior in an attempt to get ahead in life, to impress others, to feel superior about ourselves, to earn points with God, or merely to meet external expectations while our hearts remain cold. This kind of empty rule-keeping often gets us nowhere with others, who can see through it. More importantly, it gets us nowhere with God, who looks on the heart (see 1 Samuel 16:7).

EXERCISE: Again in this lesson, the exercise includes religious achievements and satisfactions among the things of this life we might be gripping too tightly. You may want to remind your group that personal satisfaction from spiritual "success" can be just as big an idol as other forms of success if it supplants the worship of God himself. And to strive for godliness without first resting in Jesus will bring no more progress than we might get from wonton disregard for wise living. "Whoever abides in me and I in him, he it is that bears much fruit, for apart from me you can do nothing" (John 15:5).

LESSON 7: LIFE

Ecclesiastes is helpfully honest about the fact that believers suffer in this world right alongside unbelievers and that, in fact, this is part of God's good plan for us. Understanding that this is normal to life—especially a Christian life—loosens our grip on worldly comforts. This in turn frees us to love others as Jesus did, "who, though he was in the form of God, did not count equality with God a thing to be grasped, but emptied himself, by taking the form of a servant" (Philippians 2:6–7). Such a life includes big and small "deaths" daily. But because it is a life of love modeled after the exquisite life of Jesus, it is a full life.

The understanding that a Christian life normally includes much suffering, futility, and sadness makes us unafraid to enter into situations that might lead to these. It also makes us willing to give away things we once grasped tightly. A necessary prerequisite to truly enjoying what we do have is that we hold it loosely rather than fearfully. "It is more blessed to give than to receive" (Acts 20:35).

The example in verses 13–16 shows that a simple but wise life has great value even though it tends to go unappreciated. In much the same way, setting aside worldly ambition to enjoy God's gifts and to care for others will often go unnoticed or fail to bring any acclaim. But it is wise nevertheless, good for our neighbors, and pleasing to God. And if we have given up grasping for acclaim, it will bring us joy. It is part of the good life God has given us.

LESSON 8: PLANTING

Although farming is this passage's main metaphor, and financial investment may be partly in mind, the Preacher surely means for us also to apply his wisdom to relationships and the people around us, which are so important. Much like planting and other investments, caring for people might initially seem like a waste or a loss. It takes time, money, and physical or emotional energy. But in the end, such a lifestyle is satisfying and the gain is rewarding.

The uncertainties of life make us more generous, almost reckless, in how we "sow" and invest in others. We don't know in whom God might be working. Investments in some people will end only in disaster. But other investments, by the secret and inner work of God, will bear fruit in the life of someone we never dreamed would be receptive soil. If we spend our time trying to "observe the wind," figuring out the best time and place to care for people by how we think the Spirit is working, we will never get around to sowing at all. It is better to sow early and often and everywhere.

See John 3:5–8 to see how Jesus applies the wind illustration to the work of the Spirit (literally, the "wind") in people's hearts.

NOTE: This lesson's Bible conversation has only two questions because the exercise is a bit longer than usual. Plan your time accordingly.

LESSON 9: AGING

There is an ominous tone to much of the language of Ecclesiastes 12, as it mentions darkening skies, dimming lights, terrors, and bodies that snap and break and shatter. There is also a sense of urgency due to the foreboding days ahead. Looking deeper, there is a feeling that we are connected to our place in the larger cosmic story, as we are told to remember our Creator, and as death returns our bodies to the dust and our souls to our eternal home with God. The passage also might cause us to feel loss, nostalgia, or many other emotions.

We should not miss the fact that this reflection on aging is directed to those who are still young. Many young people find it easy to live for what their hearts desire and what their eyes see (11:9). But certainly, it is hard to do so in a way that remembers to honor God who will judge us for sin, or to put aside anxiety and pain over things that will not last (11:10), and to do it all in a spirit of rejoicing—in service to our Creator and gratitude for his gifts.

Whatever our age, we are sometimes inclined to say that one day we will get around to serving God more fully, repenting of sin more deeply, loving others more intentionally, or enjoying our Father more regularly—but not today. To this, the Teacher tells us that today is the best day to remember our Creator. We should not wait for more maturity, because youth has great advantages. We should not wait for a more opportune situation, because we do not know what the future holds. We should not wait until our career track or family life becomes better established, because all of that is vanity. We should start today, because the dust is about to reclaim our bodies and our Maker is about to call home our souls.

LESSON 10: ETERNITY

The closing comments to Ecclesiastes give several reasons why the Preacher's wisdom is important: His words were carefully prepared. They are words of delight. They are words of truth. They may be painful to hear, but they move us where we need to go. They are necessary to help us avoid endless and futile attempts at becoming wise through the world's learning. And they lead us finally to fear God and keep his commandments, which is our creaturely place and honorable duty.

Certainly, we may also take the closing words about judgment as a strong reminder not to trifle with God and his word—to be serious about obeying him and about heeding the Preacher's advice. A warning of judgment fits Ecclesiastes. After all, the book's message is designed to turn us away from self-effort and self-glory and the pursuit of earthly treasures, and the alternative to these vanities is faith in Jesus. This is how we are saved from the final judgment.

But the sureness of judgment is more than a warning. It also brings hope. It is a reminder that eternal life does exist, that evil will get its due, that kingdom work will be rewarded, that the commandments of God are a sweet gift, that the punishment taken for us by Jesus was complete and leaves no doubt, and that our Father looks into our hearts and knows exactly what is there—including every fear and frustration and all our sinful striving—and still loves us to the end of time and beyond.

ENDNOTES

1. Alex Zanardi, "Rio Paralympics 2016: Alex Zanardi Wins Gold on Eve of 15-Year Crash Anniversary," website of the BBC, September 14, 2016, https://www.bbc.com/sport/disability-sport/37368133.

2. Blaise Pascal, *Pascal's Pensées*, trans. W. F. Trotter (Boston: E. P. Dutton, 1958), 113.

3. Billy Graham, sermon preached at Southern Baptist Theological Seminary, Louisville, KY, 1982, 5:33, https://www.youtube.com/watch?v=8PF3oqZ1lhs.

4. Zack Eswine, *Recovering Eden: The Gospel According to Ecclesiastes* (Phillipsburg, NJ: P&R, 2014), 130.

5. Craig Bartholomew, *Ecclesiastes*, Baker Commentary on the Old Testament (Grand Rapids, MI: Baker Academic, 2009), 180–81.

6. Derek Kidner, *Psalms 73–150*, Tyndale Old Testament Commentaries (London: Inter-Varsity Press, 1975), 262.

7. William Hazlitt, "On the Feeling of Immortality in Youth," *Monthly*, March 1827.

8. Iain D. Provan, *Ecclesiastes/Song of Songs*, NIV Application Commentary (Grand Rapids, MI: Zondervan, 2001), 213.

9. C. S. Lewis, "Learning in War-Time," in *The Weight of Glory and Other Addresses* (New York: MacMillan, 1949), 41–52.

mission
propelled by good news

At Serge we believe that mission begins through the gospel of Jesus Christ bringing God's grace into the lives of believers. This good news also sustains and empowers us to cross nations and cultures to bring the gospel of grace to those whom God is calling to himself.

As a cross-denominational, reformed sending agency with more than two hundred missionaries and twenty-five teams in five continents, we are always looking for people who are ready to take the next step in sharing Christ through:

- **Short-term Teams:** One- to two-week trips oriented around serving overseas ministries while equipping the local church for mission

- **Internships:** Eight-week to nine-month opportunities to learn about missions through serving with our overseas ministry teams

- **Apprenticeships:** Intensive twelve- to twenty-four-month training and ministry opportunities for those discerning their call to cross-cultural ministry

- **Career:** One- to five-year appointments designed to nurture you for a lifetime of ministry

 Grace at the Fray   **Visit us online at: serge.org/mission**

newgrowthpress.com

spiritual renewal resources for you

Disciples who are motivated and empowered by grace to reach out to a broken world are handmade, not mass-produced. Serge intentionally grows disciples through curricula, discipleship experiences, and training programs.

Resources for Every Stage of Growth

Serge offers grace-based, gospel-centered studies for every stage of the Christian journey. Every level of our materials focuses on essential aspects of how the Spirit transforms and motivates us through the gospel of Jesus Christ.

- **101**: The Gospel-Centered Series
  Gospel-centered studies on Christian growth, community, work, parenting, and more
- **201**: The Gospel Transformation Series
  These studies go a step deeper into gospel transformation, involve homework and more in-depth Bible study
- **301**: The Sonship Course and Serge Individual Mentoring

Mentored Sonship

For more than twenty-five years Serge has been discipling ministry leaders around the world through our Sonship course to help them experience the freedom and joy of having the gospel transform every part of their lives. A personal discipler will help you apply what you are learning to the daily struggles and situations you face, as well as, model what a gospel-centered faith looks and feels like.

Discipler Training Course

Serge's Discipler Training Course helps you gain biblical understanding and practical wisdom you need to disciple others so they experience substantive, lasting growth in their lives. Available for on-site training or via distance learning, our training programs are ideal for ministry leaders, small group leaders or those seeking to grow in their ability to disciple effectively.

 Grace at the Fray

Find more resources at serge.org

newgrowthpress.com